Wilderness
Spirituality

Wilderness Spirituality

Finding Your Way in an Unsettled World

Rodney Romney

ELEMENT

Boston, Massachusetts • Shaftesbury, Dorset
Melbourne, Victoria

First published in the USA in 1999 by
Element Books, Inc.
160 North Washington Street
Boston, Massachusetts 02114

Published in Great Britain in 1999 by
Element Books Limited
Shaftesbury, Dorset SP7 8BP

Published in Australia in 1999 by
Element Books Limited for
Penguin Books Australia Limited
487 Maroondah Highway, Ringwood, Victoria 3134

Library of Congress Cataloging-in-Publication data available

British Library Cataloguing in Publication data available

Printed and bound in the United States by Edwards Brothers

ISBN 1-86204-623-9

Contents

Introduction

This is a book about wilderness spirituality. It is not a manual about how to worship in the woods or find salvation through nature. It is a book about a certain kind of belief and faith that can transform the wilderness of life from arenas of confusion and fear into places of emancipation and hope. It is a book for all of us, because we all share a piece of the same wilderness.

There are as many kinds of wildernesses on this earth as there are cultures and beliefs. Our culture has a strong effect on what we do with the various wildernesses we encounter, but in the end, it is our belief, springing from our own spirituality, that brings about transformation.

Wilderness as a metaphor for life has a long and honored tradition. It is probably seen most clearly in the journey of the Israelites from Egypt into Canaan, which most historians place around 1300 B.C.E. The Israelites, under the guidance of Moses, moved out of five generations of slavery into forty years of wandering in the wilderness. Considering the terrible suffering endured in the Sinai Desert by those lost and defeated people, it is difficult for most of us to understand their belief that God was actually taking part in their struggle. But the faith of those ancient explorers was that God was not aloof from their journey but active within it, guiding and shaping the course of their affairs to some divine and sovereign purpose.

In the course of their wilderness wanderings, the Israelites found certain markers that sustained and guided them. The first markers were external, symbolized by a cloud by day and a pillar of fire by night that accompanied them on their journey. Most biblical scholars attribute these phenomena to the presence of an active volcano that loomed on the landscape of the desert, appearing as both a terrible sign and a comforting reminder that God was with the Israelites. Other external markers followed, such as water springing from a rock and bread falling from heaven. These were allegorical reminders to the people of God's providence and sustaining care.

There came a time, however, when the markers shifted from the external to the internal, symbolized by the law that was given to Moses on Mount Sinai. That shift signaled the transformation of their landscape from wilderness to Promised Land. The law was given to transform the people from a cantankerous crowd into a compassionate community, bound to one another and to God by a covenant bond. The main aspects of this law are known today as the Ten Commandments and are still moral guidestones for humanity, when it has taken the time to listen and to obey them.

As we stand on the eve of the twenty-first century, thousands of years removed from Israel's wandering in the wilderness, we realize that we are in some ways not much different from them. We confront our own hostile desert tribes, symbolized by such threats as rising crime, escalation of violence, pollution of our environment, economic recession, disintegration of our most cherished institutions and international mistrust.

In the midst of these problems, we are all looking for the same thing: a safe landing where we and our children can be free and contented. We are trying to get home.

I believe we can achieve the Promised Land, not by railing against or destroying our various wildernesses but by moving through them in joyful and deep concern for the health and welfare for our planet and all its life-forms and with a personal resolve to take individual responsibility for our own strength and growth. To that end I offer this book.

Part One deals briefly with the wilderness experience itself, from nature to death. Part Two offers twelve markers by which the spiritual explorer can move into the new wilderness of this age and find it as the route to the Promised Land. Before we can reach any such destination, however, we have to be strengthened and unified within ourselves and bound to each other by the common experiences we all share. The markers are for that purpose and are not dependent on any particular sectarianism. Although I write from my personal perspective, which is Christian, the markers are universal. They offer a kind of twelve-step program to wilderness spirituality.

The beatitudes, the prayers and the spiritual exercises that accompany each marker can be used as daily reminders of the blessings that accompany us as we journey. If, for example, one determines to travel for a week with *remembering* as the marker, the beatitude for that discipline can be committed to memory. Thus, in recalling the beatitude, we unfold the sacred memory of who we really are.

This is a book that I hope can be read not once and laid aside but read and used many times over. As I reflect on the experiences on my own sojourn in the wilderness, I trust that you, the reader, will be led to reflect on your own journey and to see your life experiences as a litany of God's purposeful activity and loving presence. The life story of one person, though set in its own particular time frame and circumstances, bears a similarity to the life stories of all, for we learn the essential lessons of life from each other.

I am not sure who invented the comic routine of the harried family member rushing home from the mean streets of the city and slamming the door on that world with the frantic exclamation, "It's a jungle out there!" But I do know for many the jungle is not "out there." It's inside. Our personal lives often look more like a snarled web of destructive experiences than an orderly pattern of connected meaning. I believe that perception can change. As we gain spiritual perspective, we can start to see that all life has a divine destiny and that there is an ultimate purpose behind every experience, even those that we sometimes call mistakes or that leave us broken and wounded. When the jungle inside becomes a place of serenity and sacred meaning, the jungle outside will be slowly and systematically transformed.

As we share the experiences of the wilderness with others and discover our common history, we will be forged into a community of people bonded to one another by this life journey and committed to one another by faith and love. It is no accident that we are on this earth at this particular time, and every person that is in our lives is there by divine design. Our wilderness is a gift. It is up to us to unwrap the gift.

I wish all of you deep peace and great vision as you explore your own wilderness.

Acknowledgments

Thanks to the following persons without whom this book could not have come to fruition:

Barbara Neighbors Deal from Ojai, California, my agent and friend of the years. She is the unnamed person in Chapter Eleven with whom I had the dialogue on the meaning of confessing. Barbara believed in my work and my writing even when I did not.

The editors at Element Books in Boston whose genuine interest and support helped finalize the work: Roberta Scimone, Greg Brandenburgh and Darren Kelly. Also thanks to Joan Parisi Wilcox for her keen insight and unsparing attention to textual details.

The people of the Seattle First Baptist Church who have listened to my words for twenty years and have encouraged me to write them down. The members of my office staff at Seattle First Baptist Church, who went the extra mile in offering assistance: Chuck Boyer, Jerri Bottomly and Kathy Doolin.

Finally, to all those individuals in my life through whom God has appeared in extraordinary ways, but most especially to Beverly, my wife and friend for thirty-six years. Without her love, wisdom and constant support, this wilderness journey would have been much more difficult and this book could not have been written.

The Wilderness Experience

A wilderness is an unexplored place. To the average person that means it is unmapped, unsettled and unfriendly. But every wilderness has its own distinctive markers and its own set of inhabitants. It is neither hostile nor friendly. It is what it is—an unexplored place that challenges and lures us away from the human institutions of civilization and tradition.

Generally, however, human explorers enter wilderness for the primary purpose of subduing it, controlling it and reaping its resources for profit and gain. Whoever or whatever might be living in the wilderness is considered expendable. Instead of respecting the wilderness for what it might offer, the explorers seek to mold and shape it into something that will conform to the great enterprise of civilization. We go to the wilderness to be free from civilization, and we end up as its corrupters by forcing civilization upon it. When Daniel Boone returned from one of his explorations in the Cumberlands, the story goes that he was asked if he had ever been lost. His answer, perhaps more legendary than fact, was "Nope, not lost but bewildered a heap o' times." Such is the way of the wilderness. It more often bewilders than betrays, while we, its invaders, corrupt and destroy.

Some years later, John Muir, American naturalist and explorer, was to affirm that the hope of the world was in God's great, fresh, unblighted wilderness. Even Muir with all his great love for the wilderness, who said that the clearest way into the Universe is through a forest wilderness, saw humanity as its redeemer. He, along with Havelock Ellis, implied that the Promised Land always lies on the other side of the wilderness, not in it, even as the Children of Israel had believed hundreds of centuries earlier during their forty years of wilderness wandering. In the same manner, John Bunyan's Pilgrim believed that true progress lay on the other side of the disturbing barrier of the wilderness of this world.

But now that we have "redeemed" most of the wildernesses of our world by civilizing them, we are beginning to take a second look at what wilderness really means. We are daring to believe that perhaps wilderness can be our redeemer if we can listen to it and learn from it before it is too late. We are beginning to see wilderness as a metaphor for life and death and to remember that the voice that cries from the wilderness of our dreams is offering us the way to salvation, as it always has in the past.

To those who set forth as explorers of their own particular wilderness, the following aphorism may offer incentive and reassurance:

No wilderness is without light,
once you are willing to explore its darkness.
No wilderness is without its friendly voices,
once you are prepared to listen.

1

The Wilderness Dream

We have all had wilderness dreams, whether we recognize them as such or not. Those dreams are both fearful and wonderful. They connect us to the exploration of spirit that goes on relentlessly in everyone. Where is my place? Who are my people? How do I fit into the scheme of things going on around me? Who am I in relationship to my world? These are the questions that haunt us and that are sometimes answered in our dreams, particularly in those dreams that feature some aspect of wilderness.

This book grew out of my dream of the wilderness, a dream that was almost augural. It came in the early part of 1992 when I was thinking about writing a book on wilderness as a spiritual metaphor. I worked with that dream for several months before I began to write, and it was a significant contributing factor to the development of thought that finally emerged in the content of this book. The more I explored the wilderness continent of sleep and the dream that emerged from that wilderness, the more I discovered wider and grander territories within myself to be explored.

In my dream, I am standing before a large two-storied house with a gabled roof. Its details are sharply etched, yet oddly crystalline. A flight of stairs leads to a veranda and a huge door. As though bidden through some inner dictate, I climb the stairs, push open the door and move inside. But instead of being in a room, I am standing on the edge of a vast field. The house was actually a kind of false front, such as you might see in a movie set. The door does not lead to an enclosed interior but to the spacious sweep of a prairie.

The prairie is abloom with tiny white and yellow flowers. Bees drift lazily from flower to flower. The long, sweet-smelling grass ruffles in a gentle wind. The ebullient song of the meadowlark, so familiar from my boyhood years, fills the air, and from afar comes the murmuring of a flowing creek. In all directions the green and yellow prairie stretches under a pure blue sky, whose depth of color is starkly accented by a few fluffy clouds. The combination of land, sky, flowers, distances and climate is so ideal it could be something reproduced on canvas by an artist whose heart has been captivated by the West.

What did this dream mean? We usually dream in symbols, which can be interpreted only by the personal association we have with the object or symbol. Yet on a universal level, when we dream of a house, it generally represents, in a variety of ways, the activities of the self. Opening a door often represents opening the mind to a new place of awareness within, the clue to the opportunity often dependent on what we find on the other side of the door. Conversely, a door that is locked or cannot be opened represents a barrier within our own mind.

What was the meaning of the prairie? Historically, it represented abundance, life and freedom. The disappearance of the natural prairies in this country, along with the disappearance of virgin forests, thus marks not only a tragic loss and a drastic shift in the ecosystem but also a loss of interior richness and abundance. When this country was raw, and before the great sea of grass stretching across a third of our nation was greedily consumed by the plow, the scrawny buffalo grass and blue gama of the prairies offered food for the many life-forms who chose to inhabit its reaches. As we denied these life-forms food and habitat, we diminished our own physical and spiritual sustenance.

The prairie in my dream was akin to the wilderness I had known in my childhood and youth. It was alive, pulsating with light, life and color, and hence an obvious symbol for my mental freedom and spiritual expansion. There were no fences or barriers in sight once the door was opened. There was only the inviting reach of a splendid and brilliant freedom. My prairie was obviously a wilderness symbol. It represented a kind of native intelligence, a wisdom more vast than any contained in a single self. I saw the dream as a sign of new areas of awareness and knowing expanding within myself. The old forms that once held me captive inside were giving way to new vistas of thought and truth. The door into the house was a door into myself. When opened, it led me into a wilderness, but it was not a frightening place. The wilderness was really a place of expanding knowing, freedom and understanding. It was a place destined to take me home.

Dreams are not simply mental chatter; they are rich resources for self-awareness. Dreams of wilderness, in particular, can connect us to our past and our future, to our losses and our gains. There are many kinds of wildernesses. Some of these are new and particular to our own age; others are older than humanity itself. We will briefly explore some of those wildernesses, after which I will suggest some markers that will help us find our way through our own particular wilderness and realize the blessings that wait for us in the new wilderness of our time.

2

The Wilderness of Nature

A coyote came to drink one morning from the creek that runs through the bottom of the little ravine on the east side of our house. If I had not been sitting silently on the bank above, absorbed in the sound of the creek and the splendid quiet that pulsated beneath its babble, I would have missed seeing him. At first I thought it was a dog slouching through the undergrowth of scrub alders and blackberry bushes in pursuit of a gopher or squirrel. But then I realized no dog holds its tail at that downward slant, especially one on a hunt. It was a coyote, part of the band, I suspected, that could sometimes be heard howling late at night when most of the human world was asleep.

Those wild nocturnal cries always take me back across the years to another place, an old farmhouse in a snowy valley. Lying in bed at night, buried under piles of blankets, warming my feet on a heated flat iron that my mother had wrapped in flannel, I would listen to the mournful wails of coyote packs coming across the frozen fields and plains, and I would shiver at the sound of that lonely, plaintive serenade. Now here was one of the singers at close range.

Only a week before, the *Seattle Times* had carried a story of these urbanized creatures of the wild who have been caught by the encroachment of human civilization and who, while accommodating to it, have continued to live in alienation from it. Watch your pets, warned the article, for numerous homeowners living near greenbelts or undeveloped ravines have reported the sudden and mysterious disappearance of cats and small dogs. The article wondered if small children might be at risk and hinted at the possible need for traps or poison to eliminate this leftover marauder and menace of frontier years. But the coyote is hardly a menace, except to smaller animals. When sheep were introduced to the western plains, the coyote became an enemy of the sheep owners because he often raided their herds for young lambs. We brought the coyote a new delicacy and then hated him for liking it.

I watched the coyote lower its head and drink daintily from the stream. Then something in the distance seemed to catch and hold his gaze. Looking through the trees, he saw the silver-blue expanse of the Puget Sound, about twenty feet below. I was close enough to see the delicate inner structure of his ears as they twitched gently, the intensity of his eyes that probed the watery meadows, the ruffling of the neck fur caused by the breeze blowing up from the sea. It was a moment not unlike that described by Barry Lopez in his book *Arctic Dreams* when he observed a polar bear lying on a frozen landscape looking across the great strait of ice and water with an expression that was endlessly arresting and incomprehensibly vulnerable, a moment so beautiful it made him want to cry. Seeing the coyote frozen in its primitive contemplation made me also want to cry. At that moment an involuntary movement on my part caused him to swing his head in my direction. Our eyes met for a brief fraction of a second. Then he was gone so swiftly and silently that I had no notion how or where he went, except that the space where he had stood was suddenly empty.

Before the European invaders reached this continent, the coyote was free. Today that freedom is fading, giving way to the relentless urbanization of the wilderness and forcing all of us to live with the contradiction of change. This modern entrapment of the coyote is a parable of our own time, not only as a symbol of our vanishing wildernesses but of an important human component that is also in danger of vanishing simultaneously. We must devise some kinder way to live with animals, some wiser way of behaving toward the land, or we will lose the essence of what it means to be human and to share life with a complex coil of species and subspecies.

The little pocket handkerchief of wilderness that surrounds our Seattle home has been altered in the decade plus that we have lived here. We homeowners have fertilized our lawns with deadly chemicals to eradicate weeds and poisoned the soil of the steep bank of the ravine to eliminate the blackberry bushes. How much damage this did to the wildlife who lived in that ravine is impossible to know, but came a hard rain and the unprotected soil of the bank slid its poison into the creek and headed to the sea. Concern that mountain beavers had honeycombed the bank with their holes, and had thus threatened the stability of the soil, resulted in the installation of an elaborate trapping mechanism. It must have been successful, for I haven't seen a mountain beaver in the area since. The fir trees in the ravine had a family of squirrels whose labors and antics I loved to observe. Then their number began to decrease. Last year we found one of them dead at the foot of a tree, apparently the last of the family, for now the trees are largely silent except for the crows. A garden snake that I saved from our cat on more than one occasion and was careful not to disturb when I was weeding crawled to my front door two years ago and died. Like the mountain beaver and the squirrel, she has not been replaced. Have we killed them with our lethal sprays and deadly pellets? Enemies of the hostile and unfriendly denizens of the wild, have we unwittingly become enemies of those who would be our friends? Or will they return as we extend a friendly welcome?

Wallace Stegner, whose significant contribution to Western literature has been to reveal how the myth of the wilderness is buried deep in the American psyche, finds it worrisome, as do I, that primitive areas are disappearing at an alarming rate. They have been plowed under by the bulldozers of technology and development. Stegner writes that who we are as a people strongly relates to our living in big, empty spaces under a great sky, in wildernesses that are alternately serene and furious. There is something, he says, about exposure to nature's wilderness that not only speaks to us of our individual smallness but speaks steadily about who we are.

With much of our burgeoning population now caught in wildernesses of urban despair, living in the horror of look-alike boxes and stranded on a planet that is slowly dying from human pollution, we need to offer a hope and a way for humanity to climb out of the wreckage it has made. Everywhere we humans have gone, we have left tracks of destruction. It is not too late for us to change. The wilderness of nature offers both a hope and a way, for it tugs at the mind and heart with a strange and compelling intensity.

Humanity's archaic affinity for the land is truly an antidote to the loneliness that in our culture we often associate with individual estrangement and despair. Yet we have in recent times begun to separate ourselves from the land that we occupy, even though it is against our own best interests. We have turned all animals and elements of the natural world into objects that we manipulate with witless insensitivity to serve the complicated strands of our destiny and desires. By so doing we have destroyed our own home, forgetting what Marcus Aurelius said so long ago, "That which is bad for the beehive cannot be good for the bee."

Wilderness is the closest thing to home we will ever know on this earth. There is something inside the wilderness—a light, a warmth, a tenderness, a presence—that draws us deeply into life. In the wilderness we find the presence of eternity, what the mystics call a timeless presence in time. In the wilderness we possess nothing but have everything. In the wilderness we learn what it means to be. We learn what it means to forgo ownership and become all attentive. In the solitude of wilderness we learn what it means to be at home.

We do not have to look very hard to find wildernesses in our lives that represent displacements. But we can also find wildernesses that have brought us to the place where we heard God's call and experienced God's presence. I have found such wilderness at the bottom of the Grand Canyon, as I slept under the stars; in the middle of a North Dakota prairie, when the wind was so strong I could actually lean against it and remain upright; at Cape Flattery, on the coast of Washington, where the shoreline is a wild and broken wall of seastacks and violent surf; in a canyon in Idaho's mountains, where walls narrowed the sky and aspens shivered in delight over a cascading creek. In those and a hundred other wildernesses I have found my place, until wilderness has come to mean for me not exile or displacement but placement and home.

Wilderness is more than a metaphor of home. It is a symbol of life itself. We enter the wilderness of life through a rite known as birth, and we pass through many ordeals in our journey toward its own center, toward *atman*, as the Hindus call the essence of the individual. There are occasions when we feel lost in the wilderness. There are also occasions when we emerge from the wilderness as a victor. Everyone has had that experience.

But life, like the world, is not just one wilderness. It is many. Once the center of the wilderness has been reached, we are enriched. Our consciousness is deepened, and everything becomes clear and meaningful. But always the wilderness goes on. Other encounters, other trials, other levels. Eventually we discover that to seek the center of the wilderness is to seek one's own true nature, or as a Zen master has said, "Your long-lost home." The wilderness of God's nature becomes the wilderness of our nature.

Ultimately all human striving and effort return to the wilderness for validation and renewal. Wilderness preservation is not only a necessity in preserving nature's harmonies, but it is also a mandate for the human spirit. We somehow need to experience wildness before we can learn to respect freedom. The human self can only partially realize itself in settled communities. It needs wilderness, for in wildness, as Thoreau observed, is the preservation of the world.

We all have a deep and pervasive longing to be connected with nature. Whether that longing rises out of the genetic memory inherited from our pioneer ancestors or from a deeper, more primitive hunger of the soul, we are afflicted by it all our lives. Moreover, we are never truly happy or at ease until we locate some piece of wilderness for ourselves where we can go periodically for retreat and renewal.

Perhaps this driving search for wilderness emerges from the fact that we are always in quest of something greater than ourselves. In a wilderness something happens to us that happens in no other place or way: We become conscious of infinity. Ask any man, woman or child to describe where they would like to live if they could, and they will inevitably come up with a visual or verbal sketch of a pine-sheltered cabin on the shores of a remote mountain lake or some similar place.

The largeness of the wilderness first inflicts us with a sense of smallness and insignificance. But as we ponder and explore, contemplate and venture forth, and as we give ourselves over to the rugged grandeur of the wilderness, whether landscape, seascape or skyscape, something grand and awesome enters into us. Our minds grow quiet as our soul expands. And in being lifted out of ourselves, as it were, we simultaneously come home to the self we most truly are.

Whether we interpret wilderness as physical or spiritual, it portrays the same reality and offers us what Wallace Stegner called "a geography of hope." It is a place to visit for our souls' good, a kind of Eden into which we must venture if we would learn who we are and whose we are. In the wilderness of nature, as we discover ourselves surrounded by the blessings of the Great Mystery, we may also discover the wilderness within ourselves and come home to our true sense of place in this universe and to our reason for being here at this particular time.

3

The Wilderness of Place

I was born a child of the wilderness. That wilderness was both geographic and social. Yet it defined the terms of my identity. I look back now on all of it and give thanks, for it was that wilderness that helped me find my place and meet my soul.

Most of us have one place in our lifetime that we call our hometown. Even those of us who are migratory, moving about from place to place, usually have a fondness or preference for one place, for it was there we felt the most contentment and sense of belonging.

For me that place was the Little Lost River Valley in central Idaho. Many maps don't show it, for it is reached by poorly maintained roads, most of which are not paved. Maps may, however, show the little village of Arco, which is located almost exactly midpoint on Highway 93, a two-lane blacktop that runs 1,860 miles from the sunbaked sprawl of Phoenix, Arizona to the ice fields of Jasper, Alberta.

If you were to drive that highway heading north out of Twin Falls, Idaho, you would cross hills of lava, high desert flats of sagebrush, with the Sawtooth Range looming blue and distant to the west. You would pass through the Craters of the Moon National Monument, a vast lava field that covers eighty square miles, so named because its caves and natural bridges, cones and terraces, and weird piles of lava rocks resemble the surface of the moon. The Craters of the Moon sits in a kind of huge bowl where three periods of eruption, the last of which may have taken place three hundred years ago, spread destruction for more than two hundred thousand square miles, extending westward to the Columbia Plateau.

As you rise to the crest of that bowl, you can see Arco about twenty miles to the north. From that distance it looks like a green oasis in the desert. Only as you draw closer to it do you see that it is just an ordinary little village backed up against the termination of the Lost River Range, an extension of the Bitter Roots, which are in turn part of the Rockies. Wildcat Peak forms the backdrop for Arco, whose cliffs have been decorated by numbers representing every high school graduating class since 1920.

I was born in Arco on January 17, 1931, when, I am told, the temperature was bone-cold and snow in the valley reached fence-top levels. Arco was then a wilderness town of no more than five hundred souls with one doctor and a midwife in whose home most babies of that era were born. Arco today is twice that size in population but is basically unchanged in character and outlook.

I began and ended my public education in Arco. I climbed Wildcat Peak with my twelve senior classmates to paint our class year "'47" on the cliffs overlooking the town. I was baptized in the little lava-rock Baptist Church of Arco when I was fifteen, and fifteen years later was married in that same church. In that church I first heard the "call" to another wilderness, the ministry, a call that I mightily resisted as long as I could. Following my graduation from college, I taught for three years in the same high school I had attended. I am one of those persons who has no difficulty in naming his hometown. It was and is and will always be Arco.

It is impossible for me to think of Arco without also thinking of Little Lost River Valley. It was in the Little Lost River Mountains, namely Bell Mountain Canyon, that my father worked his mining claims. There he met and married my mother, daughter of a rancher in the valley. It was a comparatively brief marriage that lasted long enough to produce three sons, of which I was the third. After my parents' divorce, an event I was too young to remember but felt deeply most of my life, we lived for a time on my grandfather's ranch and then moved to Arco, where my mother went to work in the county sewing room for a dollar a day to support us.

I was eight when she remarried, and we moved back to the Little Lost River Valley to a big white house that perched on the banks of the river on my stepfather's ranch. I rode horseback to a one-room schoolhouse and can truthfully say that those years, difficult though they were in many ways, were some of the most significant in my life. Perhaps it was my age. I was old enough now to have a sense of place, or at least to look for it. Perhaps it was the challenge. My stepfather demonstrated no outer affection to my brothers or me and, in fact, rarely spoke to us directly.

Surely it was the place itself that spoke to me in the strong language of the wilderness. In that lonely place, with no friends my own age within miles, I began to carve out my own identity. Alone on my old horse, I scoured the plains and canyons and explored the river meadows. I made friends with animals. I developed a love and appreciation for the glory of the world around me. Both the cold harshness of the winters and the warm rhapsodies of the summers awakened seasons in my own heart, and slowly but surely, although I did not know it at the time, there was awakened in me the soul of the contemplative and the mystic. Apart from all institutional and formalized religion I found the spirituality of the wilderness, which to this day is more the source of my faith and nurturing than is the church, which I have served vocationally now for more than four decades.

I love the church. It has not only provided me with a living, it has also given me a community of people with whom I could test all the precepts of faith. But the church represents for me the urbanized aspect of faith and religion. It is too often restricted by tradition and dogma to be a place of growing and exploration. The church would more often deny the wilderness, where true spirituality is born and nurtured, because the wilderness refuses to conform to religious rules and regulations. The church is much too solipsistic, too intolerant of other spiritual pathways, too obdurate in the face of human diversity and seemingly incapable of seeing the divine in all life and creation.

Yet from the church came the mystics, the desert fathers, the women contemplatives and the explorers who knew that truth was larger than the institution itself. From the church came the pioneers who knew that faith is a journey of the spirit and heart, not simply an exercise of the mind. In the church we have the opportunity and challenge to live out the precepts of love, precepts that must be tested in the social arena if they are ever to be valid and transformative for the world.

And through the church we have the means to serve our world, to protect its wilderness resources and to help all broken and disheartened people experience better lives and to find their way home. Even though I have often felt more displaced by the church than placed, because my theology refused to conform to its strictures, I have served it with love and good intent, for I see it as capable of doing so much more than it has yet done.

Because of the church my sense of place has expanded. I spent eighteen years in Oakland, California as pastor of the Lakeshore Avenue Baptist Church, a congregation that was strongly interracial and inclusive of all people. Beverly and I were married shortly after I began my work there, and our first home was a cottage on an acre of ground, which we shared with deer, raccoons and squirrels. The land swept across the brow of a hill to offer an unparalleled view of the San Francisco Bay and its surrounding cities, a glittering jewel by night or day.

If we have only one hometown, then perhaps we also have only one home in our lifetime—that is, one house where we really put down roots and let ourselves live to the depths. Our home in Oakland was such a place. All my life I had been looking for my home, a place where I knew I belonged, and I found it there in the Oakland hills. Leaving that place to move to Seattle was one of the hardest things I ever did. I felt deracinated, pulled up by the roots.

I went back to visit that house once, after being away for about ten years. The new owners had made several changes, none of which I approved. It was, illogically, still my place. I decided, regretfully, I would visit it no more, for I would allow no owner, however constructive, to touch what lives in my heart as bright and imperishable as if I had just left it yesterday.

We moved to Washington in 1980, where I had been called to be the pastor of the First Baptist Church of Seattle. The move was wrenching but good. It was time for me to move on. I needed a new challenge, a new wilderness. Seattle provided it. I had already discovered that, even in the city, wilderness exerts a powerful influence both in terms of illusion and reprieve. Again we chose a house with a view—this time not the bustling activity of city but the serenity of sea and mountains. And gradually the serenity of that view seeped its way into my homesick heart, the way coffee drips through a percolator, until this too became my place.

We all need the wilderness of place, a place of isolation where we can allow change to overtake us, where we can adapt to a constantly altered environment, and where we can recover from our own mistakes. It is out of that wilderness of place that I live today, grateful and serene.

4

The Wilderness of Self

Scientists tell us that every apparent bottom in the physical universe is false. There simply is no such thing as a bottom, no matter how many rabbit holes you try to go down. Was this part of what theologians were trying to counteract, I wonder, when they spoke of God as Ground of our Being? Might not the metaphor be more accurate if God were spoken of as Bottomless Mystery, a limitless sponge that soaks up soul and self? Or are we only making futile efforts here in trying to apply a finite vocabulary to an infinite reality?

Whether God figures into the picture or not, the self of every person is trapped in its own wilderness. Part of that wilderness is self-imposed, but much of it is a given of our creation. We live isolated, self-contained and imprisoned in a self we did not initially create and do not always understand. It is small wonder that loneliness is the hallmark of human existence. We are basically alone in this world.

We come from a dark wilderness, we end in a dark wilderness, and the luminous interval between the two we dare to name *life*. Yet as soon as we are born, the quest for meaning begins. Whether we set forth or return, we are dying simultaneously as we live. Because of this, many tell us that the goal of life is self-realization. In defiance of the process of dying we take up the struggle to create, to compose, to turn matter into life. When that proves not to be enough, many would tell us that the goal of life is self-fulfillment. We need to find ways to enjoy our existence. But as these two streams well up within us, we instinctively begin to feel that life itself is without beginning, an indestructible force of the Universe, capable of great good but also prone to great evil. It is the evil that more often overwhelms than the good. At this point many would tell us that the goal of life is self-denial, that if we would die to self, we would most truly live.

It is our work somehow to grasp the vision of these three opposing forces and harmonize them, to modulate our thinking and our action in all three ways at once: self-realization, self-fulfillment and self-denial. How can we do that?

There are only two things we can be sure of having at any given time: the present moment and the True Self. We are often beguiled into thinking that we have tomorrow, for example. But we do not know that for sure. We only know that we have this moment, right now. We also can be deluded by thinking that whatever expresses itself from within us is holy. The fact is that we sometimes act from a false level of self, a self warped or twisted by circumstances over which we may have had no control or that we lacked the wisdom or the force to resist.

But deep within all of us, indestructible and intact, is the True Self. It is that essential part of us that knows truth when it is presented and can love even when the person or situation is unlovely. Some would call the True Self the God Self or the Christ Self. It is that aspect within us that is created in the image of the divine, and while it can be damaged or temporarily obliterated, it can never be destroyed completely, for it is inviolate and pure. As the Quakers put it, there is something of God in everyone. The way to salvation leads neither here nor there; it leads into your own True Self, for there alone is God, and there alone can we find peace.

In my second book, *Journey to Inner Space*, I said it like this: "Every person has a human self and a divine self, or an outer self and an inner self. The human self is often contrary to the inner self, for it struggles in a world of opposing personalities and conflicting forces. The goal of prayer is to melt the conflict between these two selves and to put the human self under the dominion of the spiritual self."[1]

Today I would say it a bit differently. *I think the goal of prayer, the inner life, however you wish to say it, is to unify the total person—body, mind and spirit—into an integrative, functioning whole.* It is to unite the many selves that dwell within us into the True Self. That also ought to be the goal of life, so that as we mature, we integrate and become whole. That is the root meaning of salvation.

There is a sense in which we must be prepared to die totally to ego when we plunge into the wilderness of our identity. Otherwise, our true identity cannot be found, for one's true home is not located in the personal ego but in God. Thus far I have avoided using the term *ego* in this discussion, for it can be misleading and confusing. Psychology considers the ego to be the superficial, conscious part of the id, which is the concealed, inaccessible part of the psyche, developed in response to one's physical and social environment. Philosophy uses the ego to mean the entire person, body and mind. In metaphysics, ego comes to mean the permanent real being to whom all the conscious states and attributes belong. I once heard it called a mere ignorant child of innocence floating about in the mind of being. Whatever it is, through the door of its consciousness must pass all the treasures of God.

The term ego had not been invented when Jesus was teaching. He often used the word *life* when referring to self, and he said that to lose one's life (self) for his sake was to find it. Today he might well say that to lose one's ego in God is truly to find selfhood.

The goal of the wilderness journey is not to negate the self but to bring about its true home, its true freedom. The journey is designed to take us from self-consciousness to God-consciousness, from self-centeredness to God-centeredness, from self-imprisonment to self-freedom. Though the wilderness eventually gives us our freedom, that freedom is paradoxically accomplished only through surrender. We surrender ourselves to the wilderness of place and the wilderness of self to discover where we are and who we are.

Wendell Berry, contemporary American poet, has said that if we do not know where we are, we will not know who we are. That is essentially what I am trying to say. Until we make friends with the wilderness of our place, we will never be able to make friends with the wilderness of self. Our identity as a self unfolds in the place or places in which we are planted. As Brother Lawrence of the seventeenth century noted, "Be satisfied with the state of where God has placed you."[2] He also said that when we faithfully keep ourselves in the holy presence, it begets in us a holy freedom. This holy presence, I believe, is mediated to us in the wilderness of place and finds its way into the wilderness of self, where we begin to find the graces that we all need.

It is not by chance that Christ and the prophets spent time in the wilderness. The temptation experience of Christ took place in such a wilderness as might only be compared with the blighted wastelands of Death Valley or the Dead Sea, the two lowest spots on the face of the earth. In such a place of bleak imagery, the ambiguity of ultimacy leaps out. The depth of the wilderness translates into a peak experience, not only for Jesus Christ and the prophets but for all who are willing to go into the desert.

The selfhood of Jesus is constituted in the wilderness. In the temptation sequences, Jesus is challenged to fall back on old pre-rogatives and to abandon the wilderness. His journey was similar to the desert trek of the Israelites who, fearing the wilderness, forced Moses to tempt God by asking for a sign, once and for all, that would prove whether or not God was among them (Exodus 17:7). This kind of God-baiting is not uncommon. "If you are God, get me out of this wilderness." But to do that would remove the opportunities of grace and growth that the wilderness provides.

Every person's selfhood results from internalizing place and people in a human way. But in the complex process of coming to be, we should remember that selfhood is fundamentally a gift, just as wilderness is fundamentally a gift. God graciously gives us everything we are and have and initiates a relationship with us that will help us develop a human identity. We, like Jesus, have the option of responding and internalizing the will of God into our own selfhood, of actualizing God's aim in creating us in the first place. Or we have the opportunity of making an idol out of self and setting up our own terms of survival in this wilderness.

Idolatry is the basic temptation of humanity. The ultimate idolatry is false centering of the self, an ultimate investment in something that is not ultimate. The theologian Paul Tillich has stated it precisely: "Idolatry is the elevation of a preliminary concern to ultimacy. Something essentially conditioned is taken as unconditional, something essentially partial is boosted into universality, and something essentially finite is given infinite significance."[3]

Religious nationalism, which is currently in vogue, is a kind of idolatry. The neofundamentalism of our time, which is strident and militaristic in trying to stamp its own brand of truth on American politics and religion, is willing to crucify the homosexual and support capital punishment while maintaining a strict anti-abortion stance. Neofundamentalism is a kind of idolatry that worships its own version of truth and identifies its own limited, humanly imagined future with what it believes to be God's future. Neofundamentalism has become a god, unto whom all people not in agreement may be sacrificed.

Idolatry distorts everything. It distorts self, the relationship between one's self and another, as well as one's relationship to God. Idolatry always begins in the small and frightened enclosure of the self. The challenge of Jesus, born out of his own wilderness experience, is to recenter life in the love of God. We are not called to desert our wilderness, we are called to possess it in the only way that can bring us happiness—as a creature centered in God, genuinely free to love all that God has created and to accept everything, even our wilderness self, as a gift.

———⟶•⟵———

I ran away from home for the first time when I was four years old. The details of that experience are as clear as if they had just happened last week, yet for some reason I have kept it hidden, fearing perhaps that to share it might misconstrue its meaning. I was not a disobedient, naughty child. In fact, I was generally compliant with the disciplines and restraints imposed on me by the adults in my world. But on a singular day in midsummer, I took my first tentative steps away from adult domination and into the world of my tiny, neophyte self.

My mother, my two older brothers and I had left Bell Mountain Canyon and the little log cabin my father had built and had moved back to the ranch where my grandparents lived. From the porch of that old log ranch house, you had only to look northward about four miles, across furrowed fields and sage-mantled slopes, to see the clustered community of larch, aspen and pines that were amassed at the mouth of Bell Mountain Canyon. The road leading to the canyon wound like two yellow streams of dusty ribbons across the bar and disappeared into the cool and friendly sanctuary of trees. Between the steep walls of that canyon I had taken my first steps and spoken my first words. I had carried my kitten around in my arms, had fallen in the stinging nettles that grew by the stream, and had followed my older brothers in wide-eyed wonder into a fresh and amazing wilderness world.

I knew that some rupture had been created between my mother and father. It would take me years to understand that and to know it was probably inevitable. But somewhere in my four-year-old psyche must have been hidden the desire to heal that rupture if I could. So one day, when no one was watching, I quietly left the house and started walking up the road in the direction of Bell Mountain and my father.

What was I thinking? I'm not sure. I loved my grandparents. Their ranch was a refuge for all of us, and their presence was always warm and inviting. I was not angry at them. I was not angry at my mother for leaving my father, nor did I love my father desperately or inordinately. But I must have held a secret determination to create a link that would reestablish our connections as a family. With no thought that I was being disobedient and no clear realization that a four-mile walk across an arid land was a foolhardy undertaking for a little boy, who neither wore a hat to protect him from the merciless sun nor carried a canteen to assuage his pending thirst, with no clear assessment of anything except a nameless, naive longing, I set off on a blind compass errand across a prairie that would years later reappear in a dream.

The day was, as I recall it, almost lyrical, the kind of day my romantic nature might have invented if nature had not already provided it. The air was sweet and clean, the blue sky punctuated with a few thunderheads, and the prairie fragrant and colorful with sego lilies, yellow bitter roots and Indian paintbrushes. I recall being startled and then elated when a jackrabbit bounded in front of me, alarmed and diverted momentarily when a rattlesnake sounded its warning from under a patch of bunch grass, charmed by a hawk drawing circles in the sky, and quite content that my little trek had some sort of cosmic significance.

How far I might have gone or what might have been the ultimate outcome of that day I do not know, for just as I reached the place where the twin tracks of the Bell Mountain road diverted from the unpaved highway of the valley, a car, whose cloud of dust had been visible from a distance of several miles, came around the corner. It slowed and wavered to the edge of the road as it approached me. My first inclination to dive behind a sagebrush faded, as I realized I really had nothing to fear. No one in that valley had ever menaced or hurt me. Why should I be afraid? So I stood, small and brave, to greet whomever or whatever might wish to share a piece of my adventure.

Two women were in the car. I recognized them as Wilma and Velma Peck, whose family lived on the ranch across the road from my grandparents' place. Wilma, who was driving, leaned her straw-blonde head out the open car window and called, "Rodney, what are you doing way out here?"

Now that the question was put to me, I did not know how to answer it. I must have muttered something like, "Just walking." My reply led to her next question, "Does your mother know where you are?"

"Not yet," I mumbled, aware for the first time that what I was doing did not have parental dispensation and also cognizant that the appearance of these women was prophetic of possible reprisals to come.

"Get in," she ordered, not unkindly. "We'll take you home."

I remember crawling into the front seat between them, noticing that in the back were a few buckets and crates of chokecherries, which they must have just picked in one of the nearby canyons. I was keenly aware as I sank into the seat that I could not see anything now but the dashboard of the car and that my legs were in conflict with the gear shift, which rose from the floor like a thin black cobra. Walking was infinitely preferable to being wedged low between those two women. But I rode in docile obedience back to the ranch, where my mother received me without undue scolding and only minimal curiosity about what my intentions might have been.

Perhaps it was more than the pain of family estrangement that had sent me forth that day. Maybe it was also the first rebellion of a self that intuitively knew the day would come when it would have to walk unfettered and free on its own, at which point things would never again be the same. It may have also been the inauguration of my wilderness dream of the prairie of unshackled thought and unlimited freedom, a dream more than half a century in the making. I can't be sure even now what that excursion was all about, but I do know I cannot forget it. It remains symbolic in my memory as the day I took my first baby steps toward selfhood.

I would hate to come to the end of my days and feel that I have not been fully and truly myself. I would not like to sit in the twilight, like one of Andre Gide's characters and regret the fact that I failed to ring true. Rather, I should like to approach the journey of the last breath knowing that I have known myself as fully as possible as one entrusted with a great gift and who dared, therefore, to trust others for the great gifts they had received.

So I think Wendell Berry is right. We do not know who we are until we know *where* we are. Carl Rogers, the psychologist, is also right in saying that the goal in life is to be that self that one truly is. To do that, we have to move away from self-concealment and the expectations of others, toward a friendly openness with what is going on within ourselves and toward a sincere acceptance of others and life itself.

It is my firm belief that we will forever be in a wilderness of terror until we achieve a self-sufficient inner life with a rich and heightened self-awareness. At that point the wilderness ceases to be a place of terror and becomes our home and the way to a good and happy life.

5

The Wilderness of Soul

Beverly, my wife, has a habit of purchasing a blooming plant or an art object of some kind and saying, "It is for my soul." She reminds me that I gave her the idea when I preached a sermon one time based on the Persian verse:

If of thy mortal goods thou art bereft,
And from thy slender store two loaves alone to thee are left,
Sell one, and with the dole
Buy hyacinths to feed thy soul.[1]

Exactly what is the soul? I don't know of anyone who can offer a satisfactory answer to that question for the simple reason it is impossible. All definitions are the result of intellectual enterprise, and if there is one thing the soul is *not* it is intellect. It may impinge on intellectual matters and decision, but it is not intellect. Soul has nothing to do with ego and likewise cannot be contained by what we call spirit.

Thomas Moore says that soul is the font of who we are, and yet it is far beyond our capacity to devise and to control. We can only care for it and listen to it; we cannot manage it or shape it to the designs of a willful ego, for soul is not a thing. It is a quality of depth and a dimension of value that has to do more precisely with what the Bible calls "heart" rather than with body or mind.[2]

I had a college psychology professor who said that it is the soul that makes us human and raises us above the level of all other animals. I am not so certain that animals don't have souls. I have known both dogs and cats to manifest a relatedness, an unconditional devotion, a wisdom, a depth and value that sometimes exceeded that of *homo sapiens*. But that is fuel for another discussion.

The fact that we cannot define soul makes it the supreme wilderness. We can probe the mysteries of outer space more successfully than those of inner space. Yet without defining it, we can talk about loss of soul, the presence of soul, honoring the soul, disowning or losing the soul, feeling things at soul level, and so on. For me, the soul is the divine principle in every person, which exists independent of body or mind. The soul is that spiritual part of the human being that is related to God and that transcends both birth and death.

We came on this earth with a soul, although exactly at which point the soul enters the body is widely disputed in religious circles. I personally believe the soul enters into us at the moment we take our first breath of life independent from our mother's body. One translation of the creation story says that "God breathed into the nostrils of man the breath of life, so that he became a living soul" (Genesis 2:7). If that be so, abortion is not murder of a living soul; it is simply denying a physical organism the opportunity to house a soul.

It is clear to me that no person's autobiography can begin with birth or end with death. We each extend far beyond any boundary line we can set for ourselves, whether in the past or the future, and the life of one is an endlessly repeated performance of the life of all.

It is also equally clear to me that no autobiography can confine itself to conscious life. We put in a third of our lifetimes in an unconscious state known as sleep, and even when we are awake we can will ourselves into altered states of consciousness that place us deep beneath the surface of conscious life as well as far beyond the bounds of conscious thought.

We are more than we seem, and that is both the mystery and the miracle of our existence. We extend beyond the dimensions of time and physical limitations, although our recognition of those extensions is not always frequent or accurate. Beneath the surface of our lives is a mode of experience and a reality that refuses to be denied.

The main purpose we have for coming on this earth is to grow our souls, to help them evolve into states of moral and spiritual perfection. We have had many lifetimes for that very purpose but not all of them successful in helping us achieve soul perfection. Some of us have come to earth with very old or advanced souls—that is, souls that have had many cycles of learning. Others come here with raw, unformed souls that are in their infancy. The body is only temporary housing for the soul. When it dies, the soul will continue its journey, returning to the eternal source from which it came for rest and learning, before determining its next assignment. It may or may not be in another body or back on this earth.

I give my ecclesiastical colleagues fits when I talk this way. They accuse me of heresy. I remind them that the American Medical Association has a slogan that the price of progress is always heresy. In other words, what doctors initially rule as heresy in the medical field usually ends up being truth. My heresies do not come to me from books. They are whispered to me in the deepest recesses of my soul, and I cannot be false to what my highest self affirms to be true.

We Christians need to drop our frenzied obsession with fall/redemption theology and salvation of the soul. The soul is already saved and has been since the beginning. The soul is on earth to grow, and everything we can do to care for the soul and the souls of others, so that they will also grow, is vital. The soul grows best in a climate of love and understanding; it withers in climates of hatred, fear and oppression.

I have known people who have survived horrendous childhoods of unspeakable abuse. They not only survived, some of them actually transcended the horror and became luminous lights to the world. Others may be so damaged that well-being may never come to them in this lifetime. But the soul is what keeps them going. What is sometimes called "the indomitable resilience of the human spirit" is more accurately the strength and maturity of the soul. So we need to honor and cultivate the soul, get to know it so we can listen to its wisdom, provide opportunities for its growth, care for its suffering with extreme reverence, and learn to love it. The soul in each of us is that which is of God, and it is the soul that will guide us through all our wildernesses. We do well to pray with the ancients, "My soul, wait only upon God, for all expectation and hope is from God."

We must not only learn to love and care for the soul, we must also let the soul love and care for us, for that is its primary assignment. This requires creating spaces for reflection, appreciation and silence, spaces in which the soul will help us recover the sacredness of our individual lives and complete the tasks we came on this earth to do.

In 1965 I visited a retreat center in Southern California at a place near Ojai called Meditation Mount. This is a community dedicated to praying for world peace and harmony. We spent an hour in a silent circle invoking peace for ourselves and all people. The silence of that hour was the most powerful I had ever felt up to that point in my life. It was almost palpable. I was at several points moved to such depths that I could not hold back the tears. They were not tears of grief. Later I realized they were symptoms of the voice of my own soul finally having an opportunity to speak to me.

At the conclusion of the hour, the director of the center, an ancient and tiny woman whose face was crisscrossed with a thousand wrinkles but whose step was sprightly and whose gaze was dawn-bright, took my hand, looked deeply into my eyes, and said, "God bless thee, son. Thy soul will deal with thee." I did not then know what she meant; today, I think I do.

Since the soul has come to the earth to grow and unfold, it has a vision of what it needs to do to effect that growth and unfoldment. Thus, the soul is always seeking to provide us with fresh vision and idealism. It is always seeking to ground our total being in the life of the spirit, and it is always present in our struggle of faith. The path of the soul will always seek authenticity. If given free rein, it will not allow the concealment of our shadow, for it is the avoidance of the shadow side of our nature that has caused us such unfortunate tragedies. When we give freedom to our soul, then the soul deals with us in all the ways that not only guarantee us a safe passage through this wilderness world but will also help us complete the assignment we took on by coming here.

Occasionally, we find ourselves in the presence of a soul so great in its maturity and so enlightened in its path that the entire world will stand back in awe. Seattle had the privilege of being visited by two such souls in the summer of 1993, the Dalai Lama, from Tibet, and Stephen Hawking, originally from England. The soul of each is on a very different pathway, but the work is essentially the same—to lift the horizons of human understanding and compassion.

The Dalai Lama, who is considered the fourteenth incarnation of Avalokiteshvara, a patron deity who vowed to be continually reborn for the good of Tibet, is revered by millions as the living Buddha. He, as both the spiritual and political leader of the world's 6 million Tibetan Buddhists, has been in exile since 1959, following China's occupation of his native Tibet. He is a remarkably unimposing man who radiates an air of gentle humility. His wisdom is not infallible, which should not be surprising, since no human being has ever had infallible wisdom, but his teaching on compassion and human rights is an important leavening influence in a world that has gone awry in using violence and force to settle disputes.

Stephen Hawking is a very different kind of man. Sometimes referred to as the world's smartest man (to which he answers, "Rubbish!"), Hawking has achieved world notoriety by his work in physics and his research on the theory of relativity, which is Albert Einstein's description of the way the cosmos functions. His particular specialty has been black holes, large burned-out stars that have collapsed in on themselves, pulled so densely together that nothing, not even light, was thought to be able to escape from them. Hawking's special insight was to imagine if the origin of the universe wasn't simply the reverse of the collapse of a black hole. He is now enmeshed in attempts to unify Einstein's relativity theory, the workings of the world at the largest scale, with quantum mechanics, the workings of the world at the smallest scale.

What makes Hawking's work particularly notable is that he suffers from amyotrophic lateral sclerosis, a crippling, normally fatal disease of the central nervous system, known also as Lou Gehrig's disease. He now is able to move only his eyes and a few fingers. In 1985 he had to have a tracheotomy, which removed his ability to speak. He constructs sentences by selecting words one by one from computer menus, then sending them out through a voice synthesizer. In a newspaper interview in Seattle, Hawking said that apart from being unlucky enough to get ALS, or motor neuron disease, he has been fortunate in almost every other respect. He said the help and support he received from his wife and children made it possible for him to lead a fairly normal life and to have a successful career. He expressed his good fortune in choosing a career in theoretical physics, which is all in the mind. So his disability has not been a serious handicap for him.

The normal assumption most of us would make is that to be placed in exile, whether from one's own country or from the full functioning of one's own body, is a serious handicap. And yet here are two men who demonstrate otherwise. The reality is that the soul of each chose a pathway that nothing could ultimately defeat, because the path of the soul supersedes all other pathways. Rather than allowing obstacles to block progress, the obstacles become the means by which the soul achieves its goal.

Baptists have a spiritual principle in their history that has always been meaningful and important to me and that more than any other precept ties me to the Baptist way. It is the principle of soul freedom, the right of the soul to follow its own path. Some Baptists would insist that pathway must embody certain doctrinal beliefs, but such dogma denies the idea of an individual's religious liberty. Baptists, who are true to their history, believe that no one, not even the state or the church, has a right to interfere with the pathway of one's soul.

That belief resonates strongly within me as a spiritual principle of truth. Nothing else really works for us, at least not for very long. We so much need our religious freedom that eventually the soul breaks free from all external restrictions and flows in its own channel.

It would be irresponsible to say that both Hawking and the Dalai Lama chose their obstacles as part of their soul's growth. We cannot say that with certainty. What we can say is that they have accepted their obstacles without bitterness and have turned them into stepping-stones rather than stumbling blocks. Their examples serve as motivators for the entire human race, for the path of each of us is marked by varying amounts of suffering and pain. Pain need not deter our work. It may in fact assist us in fulfilling our "call."

All of us have walked at some point in our lives in the wilderness of pain. Whether the pain came intentionally or unintentionally, it was undoubtedly accompanied by some suffering. Pain and suffering are not exceptions to the human condition; they are the inevitable actors in the drama of our lives, and they ultimately teach us the true meaning of peace. Pain is not punishment, nor is it the fault of the one who suffers. Once we can remove the need to blame or ask why, which is what the ego does, we may see our pain for what it is, the common denominator of the human experience. We are then ready to allow it to teach us and lead us to a new place of peace and acceptance.

A deep, loving acceptance of all that has been given to us, regardless of how painful, unwelcome or unjust it may seem, is one of the signs that our soul is engaged and being given deep expression. All our life experiences are truly our private gospels, our sacred books, our sutras, our mantras, our icons. The soul teaches us to read these experiences in the same searching, reverent way we would read scriptures, to find correction and guidance.

When Jesus was asked if the man was blind because of his sin or his parents' sin, Jesus said, "Neither. It was so that God's power might be found in his healing" (John 9:3). So it is for all of us. It is usually futile to ask why suffering comes to us. The greater question is to ask, What can I learn from this experience? The soul will help us listen for what suffering will teach. Every experience has the possibility of being a place of healing and growth, just as every person and creature has the possibility of being a bringer of joy. As we give the soul opportunity to reveal itself, and as we live the kind of life that fosters depth and interiority, we will discover a new power and peace.

At that point the wilderness has worked its influence upon us. We did not subdue the wilderness by conquering it. We surrendered to it and let it teach us to live from our depths. We let it give to us the art of being quiet, of trustful listening and a radiant willingness to serve God and God's creation.

Wallace Stegner said that home is what you can take away with you. If the wilderness is to be our home, then we must learn from it and take with us the enduring lessons and sacred truths that come from its depths. Just as we must work to preserve the wilderness areas in our country, not just because of what they do for us recreationally but because of what they do for us spiritually, so we must cherish the wildernesses of our lives, because these are the places where self emerges and soul is expressed. Only as we do that can we be prepared to cherish the final wilderness, our own death, and to approach it with sublime gratitude and absolute peace.

6

The Wilderness of Death

Death is our final, and hence our ultimate, wilderness. After we realize that we live in a universe of ever-expanding possibilities, and after we have come to peace with the various wildernesses of our lives and have let them teach us the lessons we need to know, it's always hard to accept the fact that we all die. How much easier it is at that point to do what we have tried unsuccessfully to do before: to take refuge in our essential helplessness rather than to take responsibility for our own godlike powers.

A part of us is traumatized by the fear of death. Humankind has done everything possible in its five or six thousand years of history to deny death. Even though we have managed to extend our life expectancy, nothing we have been able to do has kept us from finally dying. Mark Twain said that when he died, he would like to be in Cincinnati, because things always got there about ten years late, and Woody Allen said he wasn't afraid of dying, he just didn't want to be there when it happened.

The fact is these bodies, which are nothing more than heavy structures of intractable meat and bones, are designed to die. Ever since they were given to us, they have been in the process of dying. We lose a little of them each day. The physical cells we started with are not with us today. They have been replaced many times. Eventually the body will wear out and die. We may make novel arrangements in the DNA molecule to prolong life or even produce a new species, but we will never be able to create an immortal body. It just isn't in the cards.

But something else is in the cards. There is another part of us, an invisible, dimensionless aspect called the soul, which defies death, because it knows itself to be immortal. Therefore, it resists all notions of beginnings or endings. The soul is always whispering this truth to us, telling us that we are spiritual beings dwelling in physical bodies and *not* physical bodies inhabited by spiritual beings. When that awareness sinks deeply into our consciousness, we will view death not as a going to sleep but as an awakening.

One thing we have to do as we face this final wilderness is to picture history in a new way. Instead of seeing history in terms of human bodies and minds breaking free from their chains and rising up to conquer opposing forces and forging new directions, we need to see it as ethereal vibrations and rhythms united in innumerable feedback loops, whose purpose is to maintain a relatively stable structure for the human experiment to continue. Just as each body contains the universe, so each body completes the process of universal evolution by dying and freeing the soul for its next cycle.

The *Bhagavad Gita* speaks of death in these words: "As a man abandons worn-out clothes and acquires new ones, so when the body is worn out a new one is acquired by the Self, who lives within." I would interpret the "Self who lives within" as the soul.

Eknath Easwaran, a *Gita* scholar, makes this commentary on that passage:

> *To an enlightened being, death is no more traumatic than taking off an old coat. Life cannot offer any higher realization. The supreme goal of human existence has been attained. The man or woman who realizes God has everything and lacks nothing. Having this, one desires nothing further; he cannot be shaken by the heaviest burden of sorrow. Life cannot threaten such a person; all it holds is the opportunity to love, to serve, and to give.*[1]

Jesus Christ said that unless a seed falls into the earth and dies it cannot bring forth the plant. He also said that the purpose of life eternal is that we might know the only true God. For Jesus, the purpose of life in the physical body is to discover God. When that is achieved, we are at peace with our own death because we are aware of our immortality.

To live is to die, but to die is also to live. We experience many small deaths while we are in our bodies. That means we also experience a series of new births. We die to what we were and come alive to what we will be. Every moment is in this sense a dying into life. If we are afraid to die, it means we are afraid to live. As we learn to die, which is to face the ultimate wilderness, we simultaneously learn to live and to know that life is deeply and truly eternal.

7

The New
Wilderness

We have now looked at the various kinds of wildernesses we encounter in life. Before we leave Part One, I would like to explain what I mean by "the new wilderness."

In the last few years something has happened to us. Just when we thought we had conquered and tamed our final wilderness, we came face to face with a new one. It is a wilderness created by the possibility of nuclear annihilation. It is a wilderness created by the systematic failure of all the institutions we once thought to be secure. It is a wilderness created by the accumulation of all our past problems suddenly rushing upon us as one massive problem, rendering us almost inert in terms of finding solutions. It is a wilderness created by human polarization, gender mistrust, racial inequities, and economic collapse. And all this in a time when we were sure we had solved most of our problems and were in the process of ushering in a new age of affluence and prosperity.

It didn't all happen at once, but slowly it dawned on us that our present cultural era is grinding to a halt. Religious fundamentalists declared it was the long-foretold end of the world, while devotees of new age thought proclaimed it the beginning of an era that would be ultimately transformative. No matter who is right, our present generation is a transitional one. We have one collective foot planted in the soil of an old order that is dying and the other in mid-air, trying to find some solid ground on which we can build our stake in the future.

Since social environment always informs and shapes religion, the new wilderness of our time has created the need for a new spirituality. It is too early to know the exact form that spirituality will take, but what seems to be emerging is a strong linkage between spiritual principles and issues of social justice. A vengeful, arbitrary God is being left behind for a God of universal love. True religion finally is being cast into the same mold that Jesus offered: What matters is how we treat one another, and that is determined by the kind of God we choose to follow and serve.

Every generation has had to face its own wilderness, and we are where we are today because of the failures and triumphs of our human precursors. If we can take up the ancient but unfashionable tools of prayer, reflection and contemplation, we will make it through our own particular chaos. But we do not need another how-to manual any more than we need another detailed discursive on our times. We need only to have our wills rekindled and our hopes reestablished, for though this wilderness looks dangerous and dark, it is pulsating with promise and alive with vibrant possibilities. No wilderness is without light, once you are willing to explore its darkness, and no wilderness is without its friendly voices, once you are prepared to listen.

part 2

Wilderness Markers

Veteran explorers of natural wilderness quickly learn the markers the wilderness provides. These markers offer a kind of road map through uncharted territories. Part Two will offer twelve wilderness markers that I have found helpful in conducting my own spiritual explorations. I believe these markers can help all of us explore our unsettled worlds with greater safety and allow us to continue on this extraordinary venture of life with deeper joy.

Remembering is the first of these markers. Remembering the past is an essential piece of creating a future. The wilderness explorer remembers the topography, the climate, and the places that provided water, food and shelter as the journey was made. Thus, the explorer becomes conditioned and formed by the kind of country that is encountered, for every border of strangeness calls for a new kind of uprooting and dislocation. Remembering is followed by treasuring, treasuring by attending, and so on to the end.

Each marker begins with a beatitude, a kind of logo that is offered as a blessing and ends with a prayer and spiritual exercises that are designed to help the explorer make practical applications of theory to behavior.

Before every journeyer there is always an unsettled world. Blessed are those who explore this world with faith in God, hope in one's self and love for everyone and everything that is encountered.

Beatitudes for the New Wilderness

Blessed are those who remember who they are, for they shall come home to the truth of their own being.

Blessed are those who treasure the sacred trust of life, for they shall be the inheritors of everlasting riches.

Blessed are those who attend to the inner places of solitude pulsating in their own souls, for they shall know God.

Blessed are those who confess their pain and brokenness, for they shall take hold of their healing.

Blessed are those who connect to all things and refuse all sense of separation, for they shall become one with God.

Blessed are those who wrestle with their own darkness, for they shall touch again the light from which they came.

Blessed are those who wait upon God, for they shall renew their strength and deepen their faith.

Blessed are those who give compassion to the world, for they shall burst the bonds of suffering and death.

Blessed are those who forgive life for not being all they have wanted it to be, for they shall create a new beginning for themselves.

Blessed are those who accept every person as holy and who do not burden anyone with narrow judgments or stifled love, for they shall point to that mysterious road that leads back to God.

Blessed are those who realize they have been created by love and for love, for they shall live in love all the days of their lives.

Blessed are those who rejoice at all times and in all circumstances, knowing that God is in everything with eternal joy. Through them the seed of love will be eternally resown and they shall stand tiptoe in the bright kingdom of the moment, awakening the universe with their astonishing smile.

8

Remembering

*Blessed are those who remember who they are,
for they shall come home to the truth of their own being.*

I am sitting at the kitchen bar, drinking coffee and watching the Puget Sound from my window. This large finger of the Pacific Ocean, which has burrowed its way for centuries between the Olympic and Cascade mountains, curls itself leisurely in front of my house and offers me a kind of salt-air amphitheater where I may retreat and observe life.

The water is quiet. The fishermen have hauled their gear for the winter. The big ships still come and go—tankers, barges, passenger ships. Yet at the moment I am seeing nothing, nothing but tons of sky and water that are merged into each other by a slather of blue-gray light. Even the Olympics, those quiescent guardians of our northwestern shores, have gone into temporary hibernation, waiting until the misty haze parts, when they will rise again into the air like huge elephants wearing snowy blankets. The noisy crows, who live in the tall firs that frame my water view, are oddly silent, as though expecting some mysterious visitor to emerge from the translucent shadows.

It is morning, and I am remembering. I am remembering how this spot has become a threshold for me, a threshold where I turn aside from outer images and move toward my solitary, enduring self. A threshold where I seek an essential silence, the one place in me that speaks what I uniquely need to hear. A threshold that leads me from the scatteredness of my past to the singularity of the present moment. A threshold that takes me from the unique to the universal. A threshold that takes me to the supreme venture of my days—from self to God.

To move in the direction of God is the end of what I once thought comprised my life and the discovery that the end of my wishful reveries is the beginning of my true life. So for a moment I am not doing anything. I am sitting by the window and remembering. I am remembering what God can and cannot do, has and has not done. I am remembering that I am a pilgrim traveling through a wilderness I did not create, a wilderness that has no meaning, except the meaning I bring to it. I am remembering that other pilgrims who traveled before me did not always know where they are going, and I am wondering why we are not given clearer directions.

I am not sitting here demanding explanations of God. Who am I to do such a thing? I suppose I did that when my grandfather became an old man and sat about in a sleeveless undershirt, asleep with arms folded and mouth open and adrool with slobbers. There was a time when I thought my grandfather was as much a god as man could become: invincible in strength, unwavering in honesty, unstinting in compassion. When he became old and helpless, I used to ask why. But God is not like that. God is the One who rides the wilderness wave at my feet, who lives in a universe with neither walls nor roof, who is busy at the loom of berry bushes on the bank below my house, sprouting them into life as fast as I hack them down. God is the One who is as much absorbed in the cries of the crows as in my prayers, who loves the beggar in the mall as much as the confirmand at the altar but who is also uniquely present in my own heart rememberings.

So my meditations today demand no explanations. Rather they offer an amen to God's word of grace that comes from a vast eternity to a narrow world, a word that offers companionship in the monotony of the daily routine as well as the adventure of the unexplored territories.

If God is at home, and we, as the mystics have said, are the ones in the far country, what are we to do with such a place? Tame it, subdue it, love it? Maybe we should do nothing, since we shall someday be taken from it, some yanked abruptly away before they have had even the chance to stake a claim. Perhaps all we can do is accept whatever place we are in at the moment, find life in it, that we may grow and return to the One who sent us here in the first place. Each generation has had to face its own untamed land. There is only one thing to do with a wilderness: transform it into a friendly place where our souls can grow, let it teach us what we need to know, and let it show us the way home.

As I sit here, dividing my time between looking and writing, between remembering and creating, I realize that what I would most like to do is offer a word of hope and encouragement to the human race. We are in one of the most powerful periods ever known to civilized humanity. We can make it, and we will if we choose to do so.

What I offer in these pages is a personal sharing of the moods, reflections and ponderings that have come to me as I have tried to blaze a path through my wilderness. Though our paths may be different, our call is the same. We are asked to keep traveling and trusting, even when we feel like giving up or have grown weary and fearful. We have no more reason to be afraid than did Sarah and Abraham when they obeyed God's call to go into a new land, no more than did Jesus when he obeyed God's call to leave cultural and religious traditions and move out into a new realm of spirituality. We need only remember who we are, where we began and where we are going.

That is our basic problem. *We have forgotten who we are.* Every problem we face today, every problem our ancestors faced, stems from that one simple fact. We have forgotten that we are God's children, created in love, to live in love, for the sake of love. Everything I have read of late, every thought that crosses my mind, every spiritual principle that wedges its way into my being, shouts that same thing to me. If we can only remember who we are, pause long enough to hear the call to come back to our true identity, and reestablish ourselves as daughters and sons of a loving God, we will then move out in obedient response to transform our wilderness into the kingdom of heaven.

A wilderness is not necessarily an evil place. It is, as I have said, simply a place that is unexplored. In a sense, every moment in time is a new wilderness, a time that has never happened before and will never repeat itself again. Yet the present moment, along with our True Self, is all we have. Remembering our past is important, for it keeps us from making the same mistakes. It also helps us realize how far we have come. But the past is gone. It has no power over us, except the power we give it. It can either immobilize us or spur us on, depending on how we use it. Remembering is only important if we let it carry us forward.

Jesus said the greatest law is that which had guided Israel from being a people in bondage to becoming a free nation: "Hear, Israel, the Lord our God is one Lord, and you must love the Lord your God with all your heart, and with all your soul, and with all your might" (Deuteronomy 6:4). But he added a second part: "You must love your neighbor as yourself" (Mark 12:31, Matthew 22:39, Luke 10:27). This ancient Hebraic commandment is for me, for all humanity. I must remember to love God with my whole being and my neighbor as myself *precisely because my neighbor is myself*. The point in my remembering who I am is that I might love, for by loving I find the vision and strength to continue the journey. In our collective remembering we discover that mistreatment of another is essentially a mistreatment of ourselves. We do more than remember that we are all brothers and sisters. We remember the imperative truth of our being: *We are each other*.

Do you see what would happen if we could get this truth deep down inside of us, translating it into our laws and policies? We would stop mistreating people because of skin color, gender, lifestyle, sexual orientation or differences of any kind. War would become obsolete. The so-called virtues of dominance and conquest would be seen for what they are—the brutal and tragic aberration of a species turned against itself. There would be a new celebration of love, with all caring relationships, whether heterosexual or not, fully affirmed. We would start to transcend national boundaries and link with one another globally. We would cease trying to conquer nature and let it teach us what we need to know about ourselves. Our exploitation of our environment and abuse of animals would end. We would take greater responsibility for humanity's most precious gift, our

children, and would teach them about sacred love as the
governing principle of life. We would move from our outmoded
model of a dominator society to a partnership one, which Riane
Eisler describes for us so compellingly in her landmark book,
The Chalice and the Blade.[1]

Some have predicted that as we conquer the wilderness of
our planet, space will become our new wilderness. Indeed, we
have already begun probes toward establishing space colonies:
pollution-free, demilitarized communities with a common
devotion to the expansion of human knowledge and higher
forms of existence. But would settlements in the asteroid belt
really solve our problems? Is our loneliness and fear assuaged
simply by striking out to a new wilderness? Is it not deeper,
more pervasive than that? As the circle of what we can do in the
outer realm widens, what happens to the quiet in the heart? Can
we look to outer space to give us effortless scientific salvation?
Would living in space teach us the morality and spirituality we
somehow have failed to learn here on this planet? Would we be
any closer to God in an extraterrestrial colony than we are here?

I think not. If we can't get it together on this planet, we
aren't going to make it on another. There is a spiritual element
in us that includes the whole cosmos. We are not just a part of
something; we are each the whole. And because of the spiritual
element, we are doomed to loneliness forever until we begin to
establish our connections with everything else.

So when I cannot bear to read another headline, or listen to
any more insane political gibberish, or watch the theater of the
absurd play itself out in the world around me, I step across the
threshold that puts me into contact with that part of nature that
is without, as well as the whole of nature that is within. When I
do that, my life is truly an extraordinary and fulfilling
adventure, and the wilderness around me pulsates with promise

and opportunity. Then I can pray the line from the old Scottish prayer book, "I praise and worship Thee, O Lord, for the great and mysterious opportunity of my life." These words hint at the depth and mystery we each carry.

Often as I cross that invisible threshold into that realm of great and mysterious opportunity, I am led back through the years to remember the special quality I had as a child and to those lost yet strangely alive years of searching. Life then was both beautiful and painful, yet somehow fixed forever in the mind and design of God and peopled with those who were destined to teach me something of endurance and caring.

If we do get to choose our parents, I chose well. It took me a long time, however, to realize that I needed those parents, exactly as they were, to help me find the power to live a full, adult, living, breathing life and to be what I am capable of becoming.

My father came from a prominent Mormon pioneer family. His grandparents came west with Brigham Young and settled in Salt Lake City. My great-grandfather practiced polygamy, until it was declared illegal by the state, so Utah is generously populated by Romneys. My father left home when he was a young man and migrated into Idaho to one of the lonely canyons that opened into the Little Lost River Valley. There, in the shadow of Bell Mountain, he built a cabin from logs he felled and trimmed and began to prospect for gold. He lived out the rest of his life in that canyon. The cabin still stands today.

My mother was the daughter of a rancher in the valley, the second oldest of five children. Her family had come west by wagon and horseback from Missouri and Kansas, with a lengthy stopover in Wyoming, where my mother was born. She rode horseback into the little town of Arco, at which point the family's financial resources failed, and my grandfather went to work hauling freight for one of the local mines. Eventually he turned to ranching. I gather there was never a clear decision on their part to make Lost River Valley their home. It was just what happened. By the time their financial crisis was over, they had apparently grown tired of being nomads, so they settled down to live the rest of their lives in the place they seemed to have stumbled on accidentally.

Survival often dictates the place where we live. We go where we can find work. Eventually the place takes on a comfortable security of its own, which takes precedence over aesthetic or cultural requirements, and the place becomes home. If in some premortal state we get to select our birthplace as well as our progenitors, then again I chose well, for the lonely yet strangely beautiful country where I grew up nurtured in me a deep and abiding appreciation for nature and engendered a comfortableness with solitude. Surely it was there my contemplative nature was awakened.

My mother was sixteen when she met my father, who was ten years her senior. She married him at the end of her second year of high school. I was the third son to be born to that union. Our home was the one-room cabin my father had built in Bell Mountain Canyon, long miles from any neighbors. It was a hard and almost savage life for my mother, marked by extreme poverty. After eight years of marriage, as my older brothers approached school age, she left my father and took us to live first with her parents on their ranch and eventually to the little village of Arco, where she could find work that would support us.

When I was eight, my mother remarried, this time to a sheep-rancher in the valley, where for the first time in her life she had a modicum of material security. My stepfather was a gruff, withdrawn man who was apparently disinterested in suddenly having responsibility for three growing boys, so my brothers and I often spent summers with our father. I have often wished I had known my father when I was an adult. I did not have the capacity as a child to appreciate him for who he was. In my teens I developed a resentment against him over the fact he had never given us financial support. Also, he became alcoholic, which eventually resulted in his death. Yet I look back on those summers with him as rich, life-shaping times, both in terms of that beautiful wilderness environment and his own gentle nature. He was always kind to us, always interested in what we were doing, and never let us know how much pain and loneliness must have marked his hermit-like existence in that isolated canyon.

Of all the characters that dot the landscape of my early childhood, it is Mrs. Greenbush who enters into my reveries today. She was a gnomish old woman, less than five feet in height, who wore long dresses and men's boots, skinned her hair back into an untidy bun, and smoked a corncob pipe. Since she was without teeth, the bowl of the pipe seemed to protrude more from a depressed hollow between her chin and nose than a mouth. Mrs. Greenbush was a woman without pretense or affection, who managed, in a gruff and peculiar way, to communicate a dimension of caring to those who crossed her path. It took me a good many years, however, to see it that way.

The Greenbush house was a rectangular log structure on the bank of the Little Lost River, three miles from the mouth of Bell Mountain Canyon where Dad had his mine. The roof was low, the rooms were dark, the windows small and the furnishings spartan. The long handmade table with its oilcloth covering of follicular symbols had as an invariable centerpiece a kerosene lamp with a fly-specked chimney. On this dubious board the daily fare was spread, and any unfortunate wayfarer, arriving at the door of that dark house with its liverish smell within the proximity of a mealtime, was issued the standard Greenbush invitation to break bread—except those who had the experience once would have probably preferred hunger over a second meal.

Ed Greenbush, the son, gave haircuts. If you didn't want Ed to cut your hair, it meant a drive of nearly eighty miles over dirt roads to Arco. Ed also had a peg leg, a casualty from World War I. To this day, when I think of Ed, I think of Long John Silver in *Treasure Island*, and I shiver a bit.

One day Dad decided it was time for my two brothers and me to be shorn. With no appetite for the long drive to Arco, he loaded us into the car and drove down the bar, across the river, and into the Greenbush yard. Mrs. Greenbush was sitting on the long porch shelling peas and eating the pods. The kettle into which she dropped the peas looked as if it had been lying in the yard for a couple of years and run over and trampled numerous times by the passage of various sorts of traffic.

"Afternoon," Dad yelled, climbing out of the car.

Mrs. Greenbush was hard of hearing, at least when it was convenient. She nodded, scarcely looking up from her work.

"Ed home?"

"Irrigatin'. Lower field." Have I mentioned she was also laconic?

"He was to cut the boys' hair today."

She nodded again, spitting a powerful stream of green juice at a russet-colored hen that was starting to peck too close to the porch. The hen clucked reproachfully and waddled away.

"Guess we'll see if we can find Ed," said Dad. "Come on, boys."

"Ye'll stay fer supper," she announced, as we started off in the direction of the lower field. It was not a question, nor an invitation. It was a command, blunt and peremptory.

For a single beat I saw Dad's foot hesitate in midair before he took the next step. As he set it down, he protested feebly, "That would be too much work. There are four of us."

"No work. Ye'll stay." The decision was made.

We found Ed asleep under a copse of willows, his irrigation water flooding over the banks into a patch of thistle. Ed was Mrs. Greenbush's only son. Mr. Greenbush was dead, and I never knew why, because it happened before I came on the scene. We yelled Ed awake. He sat up, saw his water running away from him, and began to swear furiously. By the time Dad had helped him remake his dams, a good hour had gone by.

"Boys need hair cuts," Dad ventured at length.

"I ain't forgot," said Ed, a bit peevishly. "We'll go to the house now. Ye'll stay fer supper." It was a statement of fact. Ed and his old mother must have had extrasensory communication, or else a common ennui drove them to snare their victims to enliven the loneliness of their table. Did I just imagine that Dad shrugged gently in a gesture of hopeless defeat? I could not yet understand his reluctance. A meal out anywhere sounded all right to me.

Back at the house, Ed limped about and drew a wooden armchair into the center of the kitchen, laid a board across the arms, shook out a depressing gray cloth, grimy from service, and called, "Who's first?"

I knew who was to be first. We had already drawn straws and I had lost. Whoever was first received the lengthiest haircut while Ed was still fresh and inspired. The last one usually got what Dad called "a lick and a promise." My two brothers vacated the premises with relish, while I climbed reluctantly upon the precarious perch and docilely permitted the formidable gray cloth to be tied around my neck, an incompetent concession to cleanliness at best.

I hated haircuts almost as much as I hated oatmeal, particularly Ed's haircuts. He was supposedly in possession of certain skills as a barber, but he must have acquired them from shearing sheep. I knew nothing of the cosmetic results of his work, having not yet reached that age of vanity where physical appearance takes on such consuming importance. But I did know that Ed made no pretense at being gentle.

He came at me with a vicious glee, flexing the hand clippers with a grinding sound that to this day gives me the shudders if I hear it, and tackled my tangled mop like it was something to be destroyed rather than beautified. No matter how far away from him I bent, Ed could reach me. Clip, clip. The clippers, dulled from years of wading through the motley forests of a thousand heads of all shapes, sizes and conditions, seemed to pull each hair out individually. Clip, clip. When I would stretch forward so far that I threatened to topple from my roost, Ed would yank me back and mutter, "Sit up there now." He went on snipping and talking to Dad, stumping around me from time to time to examine his handiwork, and prolonging the torture he was executing on my scalp with obvious pride and satisfaction.

Mrs. Greenbush came into the kitchen with her pan of peas and began preparations for dinner. Dragging a blackened kettle from the back of the stove, she dumped the freshly shelled peas into the pot to fortify some dark and indistinguishable contents already there, fired up the stove with several fresh pieces of wood, until the room was so hot you could scarcely breathe, and then pushed the mysterious kettle to the center of the range where it soon began to bubble and rumble ominously.

Clearing a place on the table, she next began the process of stirring up a batch of baking powder biscuits, and although I was certain no one could make them as well as my father, I watched her preparations with an increase of appreciation.

Mrs. Greenbush must have eaten something that disagreed with her, or possibly she was afflicted with chronic digestive problems, for she passed wind profusely and unashamedly as she worked. Once she interrupted her biscuit making to find her way outside and down the path to the malodorous outhouse. During her absence Dad tried to shoo out some of the huge flies who had been circling the room with droning monotony. He didn't have much luck. The flies continued to buzz, Ed continued to clip, and Mrs. Greenbush, when she returned, continued to emit intestinal gasses with percussive persistency.

I was finally released from my lofty spot on the makeshift barber's chair and with incredible relief was making my escape outside for a much needed breath of fresh air. As I passed the table where Mrs. Greenbush's biscuits stood in suspiciously gray molded clumps, ready to be shoved into the oven, I thought I saw one of them move. I blinked and stopped dead in my tracks. The biscuit moved again. No mistake about it. It actually swelled and then settled, as though it had drawn a long sigh. Then the one beside it also moved, seeming to hop a minute fraction of an inch into the air. The second biscuit was not only breathing, some dark-looking organism was trying to push its way through the dough to the surface.

"Hey, lookee here," I started to call out. But as I did, Dad grabbed me hard by the shoulder and said sternly, "Get outside and brush off that loose hair." He shoved me through the door, followed me out and began brushing the hair from my neck and shoulders.

"The biscuits...," I started again.

The look on my father's face froze the words in my mouth. Then he said, in a low voice, "Don't eat any."

Supper—in true rural vernacular, we called the evening meal supper—was a dismal affair. The conglomeration in the pot turned out to be stew or chili beans, I couldn't decide which. One spoonful made me think it was stew, the next spoonful convinced me it was chili. It wasn't good. Everything in it, except the peas, was cooked half to death. The peas were hard and crunchy as gravel. Coarse strips of meat floated here and there in the dark, pungent sauce and tasted like they might have been slightly tainted. Whatever it was, the concoction had obviously provided nourishment for several previous meals, judging from its overcooked condition.

The plate of biscuits was passed to me. Before I could remember not to, I had taken one on my plate. I looked at Dad with mute pleading for deliverance, but he ignored me and calmly announced he seldom ate bread, an outright lie. My brothers likewise passed up the suspicious morsels, apparently having been forewarned by Dad. I broke my biscuit open carefully, as though expecting it to explode. The interior was slightly gray but otherwise looked palatable. Then I broke each piece again, examining the wedges closely as Dad examined a chunk of ore when he took it from the ground. Finally I decorated each little piece of biscuit with home-churned butter that smelled rancid, laid these in neat rows on the edge of my plate where I could observe any suspicious movement, and took a huge swallow of milk.

The milk was beginning to sour. I swallowed it quickly and then plied several spoonfuls of stew in its wake. In my haste, I accidentally ate several pieces of the biscuit. Since no dire results followed, I managed to eat a few more bites of everything, stirring it all vigorously to give the appearance of eating.

The remainder of the evening is somewhat hazy in my memory. I recall that Mrs. Greenbush washed the dishes, dragging them through a pan of greasy water and spreading them on the table to dry, after which she sat on the porch, apparently contented, her pipe a faint ember in the gathering dusk. As we left, she laid her work-roughened hand on my head for a moment in an uncharacteristic gesture of gentleness.

On the way home, Dad explained the mystery of the biscuits. Several flies had dive-bombed the dough, and Mrs. Greenbush, whose eyesight was as incommodious as her hearing, had unknowingly mixed them in with the rest of the ingredients. The event remains stubbornly in our family annals as "the day the biscuits jumped" and even more uncomfortably in my memory as the day I ate one of them.

Today a certain sentiment, grounded in those early years, leads me to a genuine admiration for Mrs. Greenbush. She was a sangfroid old woman who was totally devoid of any false airs and who offered to all, without any apologies, the best she had. Just by being who she was she taught me something of serenity and contentment in the midst of trying or limiting circumstances. Her insouciant hospitality, once viewed as misguided or unwelcome, is a charitable ingredient found far too rarely in our modern sophisticated age. So I continue to carry a minifying spark of appreciation for the basic kindness of a woman who looked one summer afternoon at a father and his three shaggy-headed sons and announced, "Ye'll stay for supper."

In the Christian tradition there is something of the element of the eucharist in such a sharing. Where we give life to each other, Christ is present, sharing the bread and cup, for the eucharist is really a celebration of our life together as people of a common faith and mutual need.

The greatest gift any of us has is this tiny life we're given, and the greatest service we ever render is making that life count in some way for others, not just for ourselves. There is a part of each of us that always stays open and vulnerable, curious and alive, childlike and loving. The more we allow that part of ourselves to be alive and to be a companion to others, the more each of our lives will become a wonderful and fulfilling adventure.

Yet most of us are torn between a deep urge to participate in life, to allow the vulnerability, and an equally deep urge to observe it all from a safe distance. I've come to believe we must do both. We know that looking back and always wanting to return to the past is as futile as the longing demonstrated by Lot's wife, standing in the middle of the road and gazing back at the familiar city until she turned into a pillar of salt. We know, too, of the One who taught us that we are not to look back once we have laid hands to the plow; otherwise, our row will be crooked and unfit for planting. But a certain amount of looking back and remembering is essential to carrying us forward, into tomorrow's wilderness.

The wilderness always teaches us who we are and how we got to be who we are. We do well to remember the alternations of sunshine and shadow, of love and loss, that make up the life journey for all of us, for in remembering we keep ourselves from getting totally lost. In remembering who we are, we have a clearer picture of where we need to go.

The contemplative life is looking at wilderness existence from all directions. On the surface this life is quiet and reflective, but underneath it is alive with many choices. The choices we make will either build or diminish our souls. In the contemplative life we are always being asked to release: to release our past, to release our present, to release ourselves—all for the possibility of growth. The way of spiritual contemplation is the way of release. The word *release*, from the old French, means "to leave again." Release, then, is a kind of leavetaking. We have to decide what we will leave in order to keep going.

Prayer also is both a letting go and a moving forward. At its highest and best, prayer is a ritual of remembering who we are.

We are sons and daughters of God on a journey home and not just observers or pawns in a game. We can decide which road to take, which responsibilities to accept and who our companions will be as we journey. The past is always guided by spiritual memory. Words of great teachers and acts of grace and love can assist us, but we are the journeyers. We must make our own decisions, while at the same time releasing our decisions into the design of the One who is greater than anything we can plan, control or imagine, and who is more anxious than we ourselves for our safe journey and arrival.

Here at my window above the bay I can now see a small boat on the water. A lone fisherman has decided to brave the wintery sea breezes and currents. I watch him bob about, tiny and defenseless, and think of the many persons living on the seacoast who have for generations made their living by yielding to the winds and tides of the seasons. In tiny boats and fragile bodies they have surrendered to the sea and found their lives.

So we must yield ourselves to the deepest whispers and silent urges of our souls, let go of our rigid controls, and allow life to be whatever it will as it unfolds in the moment. When we yield our life to the great stream, then we do not live life; life lives us. At one level we make the decisions that lead us to where we are, but at another we are being led, encouraged and occasionally even pushed into the directions that shape our being. Life is not just a long row of randomly chained events. Nothing is ever accidental. Everything has cause and meaning. Through all of it, God is holding us and molding us to be what in truth we already are. And as our sensitivities deepen, we will realize that God is even the gentle breeze that touches our bark and pushes us toward the homeward shore.

A Prayer of Remembering

O God of Memory and God of Truth, I praise you for every remembrance of the eternal revealed amid the changing circumstances of our world. In days now gone I remember how you were revealed to me in simple folk and simple places. For love bestowed upon me by others, so wondrously given and often received without acknowledgment, I now give my thanks. Help me to remember that you call your people to live with a commitment to the building of a human society into a fellowship of love and mercy, where every soul shall find the same sanctuary of hope and strength in me as I believe I find at this moment in you. As I say yes to that call, I rest in you, letting you work in me and through me. In remembrance of Christ's love I pray. Amen.

Spiritual Exercises
for
Remembering

As you begin the wilderness journey suggested in this book, keep a journal in which you can write on a regular basis. Keeping a spiritual journal is a thought-provoking and illuminating way to record the signposts and pathways of your spiritual journey. Write on a regular basis, letting the Spirit flow through you freely. Record whatever comes to mind, without worrying about form or content, without judgment or self-censorship. Simply give your inner voice free rein. Begin with these exercises in remembering.

1. Let your memory wander back over your life until you find an incident that seems to stand out from the rest. Linger with that memory, examining it with minute consciousness and intent. Savor the sensory details—color, smell, textures, and so forth. What details emerge? Who are the main characters? Then go deeper and examine the occurrence for its emotional content. What were your responses? How do the emotions of the people involved seem to be the same or different? As you record the event and your responses to it in your journal, in a flow of spontaneous remembering, ask yourself what it is about that event of the past that made you reclaim it today? Is your remembered reaction to the event years ago different from your reaction today? Is there a spiritual truth here to be

revealed? How have you grown? Record your responses in your journal.

2. Wander back over your past to people you might have once been close to but with whom you have lost touch. With whom would you like to reestablish contact today? Is there pain or anger connected? Spend time in meditation examining how you feel. Don't deny your feelings. They are important pieces of the remembering process. Try to recognize all emotion as a gift of growth to your spirit. Record the details in your journal. Are you feeling the need to make contact with someone from your past? Write to him or her in your journal. If you feel so led, send a letter or message to the person, expressing your gratitude and caring. Often as we remember hurtful experiences from the past, the hurt will fade and forgiveness will come in its place. We will begin to see how every person who ever entered our life is sent to us for a purpose. This is the gift of remembering—the wilderness of the past is freed and given new meaning. We can journey on with greater freedom.

9

Treasuring

Blessed are those who treasure *the sacred trust of life,
for they shall be the inheritors of everlasting riches.*

There are problems in our individual and collective worlds to be
solved, and we must go on trying to solve them. But we must
learn there is also power in surrender, power in giving, power in
contemplation. Contemplation is the very ground of our being
in the world, the source of our trust. The more we trust, the less
need we have to control. The less we control, the more we have
to treasure, for our treasure will not be the prize we travel to
discover but that which we find within ourselves.

Writer Uri Shulevitz tells the story of Isaac, a man who lived
in such poverty that he always went to bed hungry. One night
he had a dream in which a voice told him to go to the capital
city and look for a treasure under the bridge by the Royal

Palace. He paid no attention to it, but the dream returned three times. He decided then it might be true, and he set out on his journey. It was a hard trip by foot, but finally he reached the capital city.

When he came to the bridge by the Royal Palace, he discovered it was guarded day and night. He did not dare search for the treasure. He wandered around the bridge from morning to evening, until the captain of the guard asked him why he was there. Isaac told him his dream. The captain laughed and said, "You poor fellow, what a pity you wore out your shoes for a dream. Listen, if I believed a dream I once had, I would go right now to the city you came from, and I'd look for a treasure under the stove in the house of a fellow named Isaac." So Isaac bowed to the captain and started on his long way home. It was again a difficult trip, but finally he reached his own town.

When he got home, he dug under his stove, and there he found the treasure. In thanksgiving, he built a house of prayer, and in one of its corners he put an inscription: "Sometimes one must travel far to discover what is near." Isaac sent the captain of the guard a priceless ruby, and for the rest of his days he lived in contentment and was never poor again.[1]

> *You wander far afield,*
> *think you must roam the earth*
> *instead of diving deep into yourself*
> *to find your real worth.*[2]

Ralph Waldo Emerson insisted that we should be more concerned with being than with doing. That thought has influenced me deeply. It has made me want to be the message itself, not just the messenger. It has driven me inexorably to the contemplative lifestyle, the letting go process. It takes years to let go, because we can only do it by degrees. But if we don't let go of the will to be successful, for example, we will go on and on struggling to get better every day, wearing ourselves and others out with our mad scramble for recognition and perfection; by doing so, we encounter barrier after barrier to our final freedom.

There is a pearl of great price within each of us, but it is not the ego. It is the Self, the whole Self, the God Self, the whole sphere and hence the center. To find this treasure of our own being we must learn to center. This must be a conscious and deliberate experiment where we hold a meeting of one, going down to the ultimate roots of our physical and moral being to seek and find ourselves—and once there, to pray. Not pray in some old, worn-out form but by lifting the soul wordlessly and imagelessly to God. Then, as we listen and respond, our oneness with God takes shape, and we discover what Jesus called the pearl of great price.

To move away from doing and toward being, as Emerson suggested, is to come to the end of much of what we once thought comprised our lives. The path we follow is often fearful and seems unsafe. But as we journey beyond the conventions that spell life for the masses, as we probe into the depths of our own past, we will finally emerge from the cave to discover once again the stars of an endless heaven.

I share here a story from my early school days in a little one-room school in Idaho as an illustration of this principle.

From the schoolyard of the Little Lost River Valley School, if you looked westward to the mountains, you could see Dead Man's Cave, a black, gaping hole about a quarter of the way up one of the slopes. It was called Dead Man's Cave because, as you might guess, a dead man had been found there, although no one could remember who the man was or when he had died. Legend said he had been a horse thief and had been shot by some irate rancher, who had placed his body in the cave. If there was anyone living in that valley with more conclusive details than that, he or she never talked about it.

The bar sloping up to the canyon below the cave was called Dead Man's Flat. It was about a two-hour horseback ride across the flat to the mouth of the canyon, and many of us youngsters had ridden there at least once to explore that mysterious cavern of rumored foul play.

One day, when spring had come to the valley and the earth was warm and green with budding things, when birds were making the air riotous with song, and when the heart of every child refused to be confined by the oppression of a schoolroom, we persuaded the teacher to let us take a picnic lunch and ride to Dead Man's Cave.

The teacher that year was a young woman fresh from the State Normal School at Lewiston, Idaho, where elementary teachers were produced in two years. Her name was Miss Penny Blossom, and that name arrived in the valley several months before she did. Before she ever made a physical appearance, we had changed her name to a half-dozen different corruptions, such as Miss Nickel Flower, Miss Benny Possum, and Walter Waymire's less acceptable Miss Panty Bosom. But when Miss Penny Blossom arrived, all those sobriquets suddenly ceased. Miss Penny was far too delicate, too feminine, too defenseless to endure such liberties with her name.

Inclined towards stoutness and manifesting a distinct air of eighteenth-century propriety, Miss Penny had a round, Dresden-doll face, milk-white complexion, and large blue eyes, all framed by pale yellow curls. Neither attractive nor homely, she was what you might describe as an adult version of the child star Shirley Temple.

There is one word that sums up a description of Miss Penny, and that word is helpless. How she ever lasted a full year in that lonely valley is beyond me. She did it, I guess, simply by being helpless. Rather than living in the teacherage behind the schoolhouse, she chose to room and board at the Byron Hawley Ranch, which had the nicest house in the entire valley, one of the few with an indoor bathroom. Mr. Hawley, or one of his hired men, always drove Miss Penny to school, saw that the fires were built, the wood stacked behind the stove, and the snow cleared from the doorway. She received privileged treatment unlike that afforded any previous teacher, not because she was seductive, likeable or infirm but rather because she was utterly and completely helpless.

In the classroom she managed to maintain control, because to have played tricks on Miss Penny Blossom would have been like mistreating some defenseless infant. She cried easily, and had a habit of fluttering her hands, rolling her eyes and squeaking, "Goodness me!" It was not that we liked her so much as we pitied her, and not even the meanest boy could have been deliberately rude to Miss Penny.

But we did take advantage of her. We told her far-fetched stories of murder and violence in the valley that threw her into spells of eye rolling and hand fluttering. We warned her of rattlesnakes ten feet long, until she was afraid to leave the school building to go to the outhouse. We told her that every unmarried female teacher who had ever come to Little Lost had been carried off by some cowboy, and we made it sound so romantic that the pathetic little thing would squeal "Goodness me!" with a perfect mixture of dread and anticipation.

But the worst thing we ever did to Miss Penny was to persuade her to dismiss school for a day to have a picnic outing at Dead Man's Cave. Any teacher other than Miss Penny would have balked firmly at such a proposal, but when we promised model behavior and described the advantages such a field trip would provide as a nature study, Miss Penny demurely gave in.

There were ten children in school that year. We all had our own horses for the trip, and Walter Waymire brought one for Miss Penny to ride. But she shrieked and jerked so hard on the reins, after we boosted her on, that the poor frightened animal began to prance, and Miss Penny, ludicrous in a pair of Mr. Hawley's bib overalls, nearly fell off in a fit of terror. I had to let her ride my old Diamond, who was gentle enough for any tenderfoot, and I rode the horse Walter had brought.

Miss Penny almost fainted from the heat before we got her across Dead Man's Flat and into the cool shade of the canyon. She had to be helped from her horse by the children and half-carried to a shady spot beside the stream, where she lay inert for nearly half an hour, her face beet red, while Ada Ruth Hawkins and Jessie Jean Mays carried water to her and kept a cool, moist hanky on her plump forehead. Finally, she was able to sit up and inquire fearfully if there were any snakes nearby and to suggest weakly that perhaps we should eat. Most of us had already eaten our lunches during the two-hour ride from the schoolhouse, and we were ready to hike up to the cave.

She shuddered as she looked up the slope, and with two or three "Goodness me's," she finally ventured to say she would stay below and see that nothing frightened the horses. We knew better than to trust her with that responsibility, and we eventually persuaded her to attempt the short climb to the cave by promising her a spectacular view of the entire valley and interesting rock formations in the cave. Thus, with much assistance from the bigger students, and after many long rest periods, Miss Penny finally huffed and puffed her way up to Dead Man's Cave.

The cave went back only a few feet, but its ceiling rose above our heads into an unpenetrable darkness. It was cool inside, and we all sat down. Miss Penny had rallied now and spoke with greater energy and enthusiasm as she oh'd and ah'd over the view, exclaiming several times, "Goodness me, it's a pretty country after all. Who would have ever believed it?"

Then Miss Penny saw some black mounded heaps along the bottom of the cave floor, and suddenly she became the school-teacher again. "Why, whatever have we here? Goodness me, this looks like some mineral deposit." She picked up a handful of the stuff and began to examine it carefully.

Walter Waymire and Jake Little had backed away with broad grins, and even Ada Ruth and Jessie Jean turned away to hide their smiles. The younger children, however, gathered around her in naive interest.

"Gee whillickers," exclaimed little Bobby Karns, the only first-grader, "maybe it's oil. My gran'daddy found oil in a cave once."

"I don't think it's oil," said Miss Penny thoughtfully, "but it is certainly something that should be analyzed. I will not be satisfied unless we take some of it back with us. Children, fill your pockets and lunch pails. I think we have made an important discovery that could have significance for this entire valley."

Walter and Jake had by this time staggered outside and were rolling on the ground, howling hysterically, and Ada Ruth and Jessie Jean had also followed them out to conceal their giggling. Those four were the oldest in the school and seemed to be in on some joke that excluded the rest of us.

"We've got to tell her," said Jessie Jean, wiping her eyes.

"Never!" gasped Walter. "It's too funny to be true!"

I had come out of the cave to see what they were doing and heard their conversation. I was only a fifth-grader then and not quite in the full center of their confidence. Walter looked at me and warned, "An' don't you tell her, neither."

"What is that stuff?" I asked, and my question sent all of them into more gales of laughter.

Just then Miss Penny and the other children joined us. She was wiping her hands fastidiously, and the pockets of her big overalls were bulging. "My, that substance is sticky," she remarked. "Well, children, let's start back."

We arrived back at school a little late, and Mr. Hawley's hired man, Scrub Haight, was waiting to take Miss Penny home. She marched straight up to him and began to remove the black chunks from her pockets.

"Mr. Haight, the children and I found this mineral up in a cave. Do you have any idea what it might be? We brought back quite a lot of it with us in case it is valuable, although there are still large quantities of it in the cave."

Scrub looked at those dainty, plumpish hands clutching the black nuggets, and he began to cough violently. His face turned red, and he backed away, choking.

"Goodness me," declared Miss Penny. "Someone better get Mr. Haight some water."

He gestured helplessly and, when he could finally manage to talk, said weakly, "Ma'am, I don't think you want that."

"Why not? Do you know what it is? I would like to have an analysis run on its content," Miss Penny said in a decisive tone.

"Ma'am," stammered Scrub, "that there is bat droppin's."

Miss Penny looked totally uncomprehending. "Bat droppings?"

"Yes, ma'am." Then seeing that she did not understand, he continued, apologetically and red-faced, "Ya know, like—er—ah manure." He pronounced it "manore," and, as he said it, he turned away with another coughing spell.

Miss Penny looked down at her hands, and the expression on her face slowly began to change from expectancy to revulsion.

"Dead Man's Cave is full o' bats, ma'am," continued Scrub. "You kids knew that," he said to us reprovingly. "Ya shoulda told her." He turned back to Miss Penny, but Miss Penny was not there.

She was moving toward the schoolhouse as rapidly as the baggy overalls would permit. Her arms were stiff at her sides and both chubby hands were twitching frantically in what appeared to be an effort to empty themselves. I caught a glimpse of her face. It was a faint shade of green. I hoped she was not going to be sick right there in front of us.

Little Bobby Karns had opened his lunch pail, which was stuffed full of the black substance. As Miss Penny disappeared into the schoolhouse, Bobby, utterly frank and wise beyond his years, said with complete disgust, "My God, I got a whole lunch pail full o' bat turds!"

Miss Penny Blossom never mentioned the incident again, and I suspect she has done her best to block it from her memory forever. As for me, I still chuckle when I think of the treasures we brought back from Dead Man's Cave that day and how in childish ignorance we made the error of assigning value to something that was utterly worthless.

Years later I came across an article in a magazine that told of the rich fertilizing content of bat guano and how it also makes possible the existence of certain lower forms of life in caves. That article took me back to Dead Man's Cave and Miss Penny Blossom, and I realized that the entire process of life is geared to teach us to assign the proper values to everything. There was no actual treasure in Dead Man's Cave that day for us. But to reflect on that innocent excursion from the land of my childhood has been and continues to be a pearl of great delight and has led me to the spiritual principle I call treasuring.

A treasurer is one who takes care of the resources of a group for the good of all. The first step in treasuring is choosing one's self. Kierkeggaard used this phrase to affirm the responsibility each has for one's self and one's existence. It means that we accept the particular spot where we exist in this universe and our responsibility for our existence in that spot. Treasuring is moving beyond self-preservation and self-fulfillment to creative self-giving, an unreserved plunge into the unknown where we give our lives away instead of a retreat into the cave where we grasp life and try to keep it for our own.

Treasuring one's self is a risk, for faith also means treasuring one's world and all that is in it. To do this, we have to learn new responses. We must learn not to resist a fall or an attack but to meet it and swing with it. We must learn to face the new wilderness of our time without fear and paranoia and in full confidence that God will lead us if we trust and obey. Treasuring means letting life lead us, instead of exerting our energy to direct life. It means joining the festivities of life instead of trying to redirect and manage them.

Many in our world today are burdened by the moment-to-moment responsibility of trying to manage themselves and others around them. Such responsibilities are tedious and energy-sapping. Again, it is our desire for control that drives us.

A better way is to know that we are carried on great winds, the winds of God, and that there is a season for ripeness within each of us. We are to let the seasons come in their own time and allow their mysterious power to change us and others. This doesn't mean we do nothing. We shall be busier than ever if we allow God to have control over us. But we shall cease demanding that life be anything other than what it is. We shall find life by releasing ourselves into it, by losing ourselves to it, as Jesus suggested, by treasuring it for the unique and precious adventure it is.

We are at our best when we comprehend and integrate the world within us with the world beyond us. It is then that we are most actively and creatively involved with life. It is then that we are moved to act in love toward ourselves, toward others and God. But the precondition of love is a state of being that is subjective rather than objective. Instead of seeing ourselves as an object in a world of objects, where we pursue ideas and thought systems, seek emotional harmony, and plunge ourselves into activities that will give us satisfaction, we need to draw back into a state of profound consciousness now and then where we can look at life simply, quietly and openly. This is a subjective state rather than an objective one.

This posture might be described as that of a small child in a crowd who pushes through a tangle of legs to stand on the sidelines and watch silently with open eyes all that is happening. This stance should be a prelude to action. For a few moments we are the beholders of the stage where human aspiration and endeavor are acted out, and in that contemplative position we ring up the curtain on spiritual consciousness and awareness.

To treasure something means to keep it as precious. When we treasure our lives, we take time to become elementally human, to be awake, to observe the wider picture, before we try to think, love or act. Seeing, awareness, being—these are the preconditions to loving, creating, doing. Treasuring is that state where we offer ourselves as the seeing and knowing eyes of the whole creation and learn to treasure the life that moves around us.

Veteran explorers of life's wilderness tell us that we must finally learn to love all persons. While a part of us cries out against such an impossibility, another part of us declares it is absolutely necessary. If the bat guano we brought back from the cave taught me anything, it is this: Something that appears disgusting, revolting or worthless has meaning and value at another level. It only needs validation in order to be treasured. Bat guano is treasure to the microorganisms that take life from it. In the bigger picture of life, everything has meaning. Discovering that meaning is the secret of treasuring it.

Before we can treasure we must be awake. Only if we are spiritually awake, can we love all things unconditionally. Modern Christianity talks a great deal about loving but very little about awakening people so they can love. Love must proceed from an awakened consciousness; otherwise, the love dwindles into sporadic acts of half-hearted goodness and benevolent pity.

The times in our wilderness journey when we draw back from existence and do nothing are times when we draw back into ourselves. This is what the contemplative life requires: reflection. We are so driven to believe that our worth as a person comes from our doing that we are afraid if we do nothing at all we shall fail. But why do we think we should succeed in everything? Whence came the notion that we must accomplish great deeds in this life before our lives can count for anything? It takes far greater courage and will to *be* than to *do*. It takes far greater effort to treasure than to reject. Treasuring is the act of finding the good that lies dormant in everything. Treasuring is the act of recovering our being from the cave of illusion and darkness so that we can act wisely in the world. Treasuring is savoring and tasting our own resources so that we can live worthy of our greatness and thus serve the common good of all.

More is required from us, however, than resting and reflecting. The soul needs periodic times of rest, where it can awaken to greater clarity, vividness and perception. But soul growth comes only through struggle. Our consciousness is restricted by many biases, such as jealousy, greed, pride, envy, hate. These are enemies that confine and weaken all of us, keeping us partially asleep. When we come to God seeking purification of self, we are acknowledging that by our own powers we cannot get freed from our baser motivations and darker instincts. Only God can do that for us.

But God cannot do it unless we are open, as open as a cave for school children on a treasure-hunting expedition. This is the whole aim of spirituality: to become open. Openness requires honesty and trust, an admission of what is wrong and a trust that God has the power to mend and heal. Openness and trust on our part will bring about the transfiguration that will help us grow large enough to receive the abundance that God is waiting to give. Having received the gift of Godself, we then grow strong enough to move back out into the world and deal with life's struggles, struggles that are there to help shape the outlines of our souls.

We are each on a path that no one has ever trod before. We are each searching for the buried treasure that is inside. We are each hoping we can make our way through this new wilderness and not lose our way or misuse the vital resources on our path. Wilderness explorers need to learn to be lost comfortably. How else shall they know the joy of homecoming?

A Prayer of Treasuring

Reveal to me today a little more of the meaning of life, that I may learn to treasure its rich variety. You who have given me so much, give me now one thing more: a grateful heart, from which shall rise my finest gifts and my dearest treasures, returned to you for your blessing and keeping. Deepen within me the invisible treasure of your own love, that in its discovery I might illumine some of the darkness and loneliness of this world. God, you are the greatest treasure I have. You cover me with kindness and care. You are the life within, the air I breathe, the food that sustains me, the water that renews and cleanses me. You are my home, in you I live and move and have my being. Thank you, Dear One. Amen.

Spiritual Exercises for Treasuring

1. Close your eyes and hear with your inner ears the sound of the word *treasure*. What does the word mean to you? What feelings and emotions does it evoke? Ask yourself, what do I treasure today? Is my treasure chest today filled with treasures different from those that once filled it? If so, how and why have my treasures changed? List in your journal the treasures that are in your chest today and those you want to take with you on the journey ahead? What are you leaving behind? Why?

2. As you may have already understood, our treasure chests are our hearts, for there we store that which is most precious and valuable to us. But occasionally we need to take inventory and consciously discard the clutter or the trash. Meditate on the scripture verse, "Where your treasure is, there will your heart be also." Repeat the verse aloud several times and ask Spirit to reveal its true inner meaning. Consider how full or empty is the treasure chest of your heart. Give thanks if it feels full. If it's empty, consider the fact that you may have been given treasures you didn't recognize. Add them to your treasure chest by listing them in your journal.

3. Lie or sit comfortably and sense your heartbeat and the pulsing of blood through your body. Feel and visualize each indrawn breath as the tide of life bringing you a treasure. With each inhalation, draw in the treasures you have identified in the first two exercises, and receive others you may not have noted before. Bring to your consciousness the things you consider to be true and lasting treasures of your life. As you exhale, let your breath carry away any "false" treasures you may have been storing. Perhaps what was once a treasure may no longer be one. Let it go, giving thanks as you do.

10

Attending

Blessed are those who attend *to the inner places of solitude pulsating in their own souls, for they shall know God.*

"He is a person with no center." Such a judgment, which we have all either leveled at someone ourselves or heard others level, sounds like the worst kind of indictment. Surely everyone has a center, although they might not know it. Those who don't live from the surface of life, taking all their cues from the world around them and allowing exteriors to determine their interiors, such as their moods and responses.

Being uncentered is not an uncommon ailment. In fact, it is more the norm than the exception. The problem with such a lifestyle is that if the outer world is chaotic and frenetic, the inner world will become the same. A person failing to live from the innermost center of his or her life is like a thermometer that registers only the changing temperature of the environment, rather than a thermostat that helps regulate and stabilize temperature.

Our centers hold the same wisdom and strength that sustain all of life everywhere. Our centers are the place of "Christ in you, the hope of glory" that the Apostle Paul talked about. Our centers are the places where we feel created yet at the same time inchoate, impaled on divinity while also incised in humanity.

We do not create our center by correct thinking, self-manipulation, or strenuous effort. Our center is created for us by the One who gave us life. We do not find it by reading books or listening to spiritually wise people. *We find our center by following the practice of attending.* We attend to the rhythms of life pulsating through us. We attend to the inner places of solitude in our own being. We attend to the life and the truth that we already have, which is within us at the center of our being. We attend to the boundaries of the self by taking the inward journey, for it is always the interior that calls when we are fine-tuned to hear and willing to take the journey beyond familiar landmarks.

We are not after success or peace of mind when we attend. We are after meaning, after glory, after God. So we use the same critical and contemplative disciplines to examine God as we use to examine what God creates. We look at God in the same mute, pondering way we would look inside a rose. We do not brush aside a single detail of the malefic imbecility that we encounter in the shadows of the wilderness, but we explore these with the same love by which we have felt ourselves embraced. We use the discipline of attending not for the sake of the discipline but in order to embrace God in return, and thus to embrace God's creation. The essence of faith does not lie in entertaining some particular concept of God but in the ability to articulate a memory of moments of illumination by God's presence, moments when we knew God was attending to us.

Seekers in the Middle Ages had a peculiar way of attending. They withdrew from the traffic of life in order to contemplate God and the mysteries of existence, giving themselves totally to lives of sacrifice and prayer. They were called anchorites (from the Greek, *anachoreo*, meaning to withdraw to a place apart). They occasionally lived in little huts fastened to the outside walls of a church. These huts, called anchorholds, had a small window through which the anchorite could look out on the sights and sounds of the world as fuel for prayer and contemplation. The sheds were hooked to the church on one side, held fast by spiritual tradition, and open to the world on the other side, drawn into the moisture of the world's pain that seemed impermeable and perpetual.

These measures seem complex and extreme to us today, but something of the anchorite existence still captivates. We can make any place we choose an anchorhold. It can be our living room, our yard, our desk, our car. Wherever and whenever we attend, we have created an anchorhold.

I live on a bluff above the Puget Sound where I can lift up my eyes to the lofty majesty of the Olympic Mountains. I can, that is, when rain clouds and foggy mists will allow. But whether the blue sky streams over my world-side window and helps me see the mountains against which I can heave my spirit, or whether inclement weather decrees the uncertainty of vision and the dissolution of the mountains, it is all the same. It is not necessary to comprehend the peaks by climbing them. It is not even necessary to see them. It is only necessary to look, and by looking one is lifted and led beyond the farthest horizons to an aim that is already present within us, though yet hidden from our sight.

The spiritual practice always has this element of simplicity. Attending is like returning again and again to the rhythm of breath and heartbeat that make up the central mystery of our bodies, in the way the Buddhists do when they meditate. Attending is a simple uniting of breath and "sacred words" as the Hindus do when they chant their mantras. Or as the Christians do when they repeat the Jesus prayer, "Lord Jesus Christ, have mercy upon me." Attending is lifting up one's eyes and heart for the long look.

None of these practices requires moral or physical effort. It is simply giving attention to the gracious mystery that lies close to our breath and pulse. It is simply participating in the quiet rhythms that move in the seas and in the stars, in the first breath of a newborn baby and the last breath of a dying person. Attending is turning to God, who is the breath-spirit in all that is.

Thomas Merton spoke of the tremendous action of contemplation, where all is attentiveness to what is happening. Carlos Castaneda is told by Don Juan, his shamanic mentor that seeing is not doing. He also advises Castaneda to look for the holes in the world and to listen to the spaces between sounds. Jesus spoke of those who have eyes but see not and who have ears and hear not. This is something of what I mean by attending. One learns to look for what is not seen with the eyes and to listen for what is not heard by the ears.

Did you learn to read from the Dick and Jane reading primers, as I did? If so, do you remember the first words you learned?

SEE.
SEE DICK.
SEE DICK RUN.
RUN, DICK, RUN.

Almost everything we need to know is there somewhere in that little word SEE. Awareness. The Golden Rule. Love and caring. Ecology and politics. Sane living. Life in harmony with the true order of things. Life in God, where life is eternal.

Let me illustrate what I am talking about with a meditation that I have sometimes used for myself as one method of centering. Visualize the world in which your life takes place as similar to the rings of a tree if you were to cut through its bole, or as similar to the ripples set in motion in a pond when a stone has been tossed into it. Within each of these rings is a certain dance for you to do that relates critically to your life. It is the dance of attending.

The large outer ring is a place filled with chaos, frenzy, turbulence. This is the outer world that encompasses you—a vast sea of negatives, anxieties and fears. The dance in this ring is a jerky, frenzied, madcap scramble, lacking rhythm or pattern. It is a scramble of avoidance and encounters with people and situations over which you seem to have no control. You find yourself running into the people you want to miss and missing the people you want to be with, as you hurtle about in a confused, feverish fashion.

Within that large ring is a smaller one, and this is the world of your responses to the outer ring. In this second circle are clearly mirrored your alarms, excitements, disappointments, dismays and heavy fears. Contrary to the previous ring, here you have some control, for you are the choreographer. But the dance is not to your liking, even though you have devised it. It is too exhausting, too debilitating, for this is the world where others are watching you, assessing your responses, gauging your reactions.

Step from that second ring into a yet smaller circle. This is the ring of your awareness of yourself, the place of your own self-consciousness, your feelings of inadequacies and ignorance. This is the place where, even as you are aware, you are aware that you are not totally aware. The dance is slower now but muted with a longing, with aching discontent. You long for something more.

Move from that ring into the next smaller ring. Here you step into a place of comparative calm and temporary peace. This is the realm where you are usually able to achieve surcease from the battering storms of the outer ring through certain external stimuli. This is the part of being that responds to great music, feels peace beside the ocean or in the mountains, worships God in a cathedral, rejoices in the supportive love of your dearest ones. This is also the realm where you often feel motivated to help others, although you are occasionally frustrated because your help does not seem to be enough.

Many believe when they reach this ring that they have found the ultimate fortification against the outer rings of precipitant activity, or at least a temporary fortress. So for many the dance stops here. But this place is too fragile, too frail, too vulnerable. Something tells you there must be another step.

Your challenge now is to step on through all the rings until you come to the very center of the concentric pattern. Here is the pebble itself that was tossed into the pool and that set in motion the outer waves now lapping against the far edges of the universe. Here is the eye of the storm. Here is the center of the tree. It is a place of absolute silence that remains unperturbed by the fury and destruction pounding at its circumference. This is the Still Point, the place where you are one with yourself and all that is. This is the place where you find the *I am* of your being. Here you find God, not the God of a church service or some theological textbook, not the God of your parents' faith, but the

God who is closer to you than hands and feet, nearer than your own breathing.

You have been here before in the great moments of your life, but those times were fleeting and transitory. You longed to recapture the experience, but you did not know how. Now you know. Through absolute quietness and a deliberate silencing of all outer things, through attending, you may dance your way into that Still Point within yourself, where you are lifted above all the rings into an eternal vision of Life as it truly is. Here the Dance dances you, propelling you gently into a rhythmic harmony that pulsates with the rhythm of the universe. You are freed from all sense of effort and responsibility, as you give yourself to the graceful flow and perfect pattern of this Dance that is carried on at the center of your being. For slowly you discover that *the dance is you*!

Now you begin to realize a new strategy and wisdom for dealing with your work and the people in your world. You sense a strong current of courage and power rising within you that is helping you transmute your dislikes and annoyances into love. All impulses to criticize, to judge harshly, to hurt, to hate are swept from you as you dance in that pinpoint of stillness; for it is not the body that dances now, it is the soul.

Now that you have found this center of the ring, your holy of holies, hold to it until you can feel serenity begin to take charge. Then move forth into the outer rings to uplift your responses, to enhance your awareness, to bring order and peace, even to the seemingly random and rhythmless outer ring that surrounds all the others. Gradually you will set in motion the Dance of healing and hope throughout all the rings of life.

Now that you have found the way, you will want to come often into that holy stillness and be lifted above everything. You will reach this Still Point when you are one-pointed in your thoughts and desires, wanting it above all other things. You will rise from such moments with a strong sense of dominion over yourself and the circumstances of your life, for these are the moments when you know yourself to be a holy son or daughter of the Most High, when the purple robe of royalty is laid upon your shoulders and the scepter placed in your hands as a symbol of your divine authority. You will return to your world to rule wisely, lovingly and beneficently, so that all creation will be blessed by you.

What you have done in these few moments is that which Jesus asked you to do: "Seek ye first the Kingdom of God and its righteousness." Your work now is to hold that kingdom, to allow no emotions, personalities or destructive elements to send you back into the mad, frenzied dance of the outer circle without a spirit of calm and order. Visit the Still Point often, for it is your place of safety and protection. It is there that you abide in the Spirit and the Spirit abides in you, so that even through the valleys of the shadows you will not be alone.

Attending, then, is dancing to the center in order to see life from within rather than from without. It is looking at life as a mystery but at the same time receiving it as a gift. It is seeing creation as painful yet also accepting it as holy. Attending is taking the long look, and then responding in ways that are loving and compassionate.

We sometimes learn the most about the value of attending when we recognize where we have failed to live up to it. To that end let me tell you about Clayton Hall, an oversized, slouchy kid with a mop of black, stringy hair that usually hung down over his small squinty eyes. Clayton was poor, and Clayton was not overly bright. Those conditions obviously could be forgiven, for they came about through no real fault of Clayton.

But Clayton was also a bully, and it took me longer to forgive that.

Life had dealt harshly with Clayton, which is why he retaliated by hurting things around him, such as June bugs, which he would squash between his grimy palms; flies that he would de-wing and drop down the back of Ada Ruth Hawkins's dress; and one ten-year-old that he would punish in various ways—me.

For almost a year Clayton was my nemesis. Periodically I went home with a swollen lip, a twisted arm or an empty lunch pail (as well as an empty stomach) because Clayton had eaten my lunch. I bore it all with outer indifference, but boiling fires of hatred were being steadily stoked within me by his constant abuse and torment.

One day the mouse roared. Clayton pushed me across the fine line that divides reason from instinct. I came into the schoolroom during recess and found him blotting ink all over a penmanship paper I had just finished. I, the meticulous and careful little student who wanted only to be left alone to pursue my intellectual interests, felt fury rising within me like bitter gall. With no thought of possible consequences, with nothing but gut-gripping, white-hot anger pressing into every cell and atom of my being, I doubled up my fist and popped Clayton in the nose with all my might.

"God damn you, Clayton, I hate you!" I yelled, all the repressed rage suddenly unleashed.

Blood spurted from Clayton's nose like a geyser, and Clayton did an amazing thing. He let out a yell of pain and mortification and ran from the schoolroom, as though he was afraid I would hit him again.

I was too stunned to realize all that had happened in that moment. Then some of the other students came running in from outside with tense, eager faces. "What did you do to Clayton?" asked one. "He's gone home on the run!" cried another.

I realized I had defeated the foe. I also realized that bullies are essentially cowards, and Clayton, the coward, never bullied me again. I rode the crest of victory proudly, and then, as often happens, the oppressed, when freed, becomes the oppressor. Hungry for conquest, I looked around for new worlds.

Martin was a slender, slightly frail boy with a perpetually runny nose. We sometimes rode our horses to school together. Martin liked me. Too bad for Martin. He was fated to taste the dregs of abuse I had suffered under the regime of Clayton Hall, now deposed.

One night after school as we walked out to the barn to our horses, I challenged Martin to a fight. At first he thought I was joking; but I grabbed him and threw him down in the snow. His expression was not one of fear—it was one of bewilderment and betrayal. To this day I can see Martin's face, and I can remember the sick feeling that suddenly gripped me. How often I have wished I could go back across the years and do just one thing that day I did not—help Martin get up out of the snow. I wish I had done something to make the helpless, hurt look on his face go away. But I didn't. I just turned and walked away, deeply ashamed but infinitely wiser.

The lessons I learned from that experience have been deeply imprinted on my consciousness. I discovered that in hurting Martin I hurt myself. I also discovered that the price of hating Clayton was to love myself less. Clayton was still the victor over me, because the thing I so loathed in him had come to rest in me. And I also learned that it takes a great deal of courage and wisdom to keep from giving out the pain that has been given to us in the first place.

Clayton and I, after a manner of speaking, became friends. At least we learned to tolerate each other. I began to see him in a new light and with a new sympathy.

The Hall family had moved into our valley one summer and taken up residence in an old abandoned house that set out in the middle of a flat. Never much of a place to begin with, it soon became worse. Old Man Hall (I never heard him called anything else) went around the valley offering himself as a hired hand. Several ranchers gave him work out of sheer pity, but he had a well-deserved reputation for having not only "the slows" but "the go-backs," valley terms that branded him as shiftless and perniciously lazy. Old Man Hall looked like his place, ramshackle and almost demolished.

Mrs. Hall, I think her first name was May, was always, in local vernacular, either hatching or sitting on the nest. There was usually a baby somewhere around. I can't even remember how many Halls there were. They seemed to go on forever. Clayton was the oldest. It wasn't until some years later that I knew that part of what was wrong with Clayton was not only the impecunious circumstances that surrounded him but that Old Man Hall liked to use his kids as punching bags. Today he would be arrested for child abuse. But back in those days it was generally believed that sparing the rod only spoiled the child. So if Clayton or his siblings came to school occasionally with welts across their legs, bruises on their arms or a blackened eye, it was probably a mark well deserved, or so we must have reasoned.

Clayton and I landed in the eighth grade together. Actually, Clayton should have been on his way at least three years earlier, but he kept repeating grades until I finally caught up with him. The teacher that year was Mrs. Harmell, a tall handsome woman with a warm smile and a dedication to teaching. She seemed to have a heart of compassion for the Halls that saw beyond their tattered condition to the fact they had been penalized by life before they even arrived. She treated all of them with a special kind of respect that left a profound impression on the rest of us, who had long been accustomed to looking down on the Halls as the valley pariahs. Clayton adored her, and for the first time, he settled down and tried to figure out what was inside a book besides pictures.

Mrs. Harmell took to placing me with Clayton to help him study. I labored with him through his arithmetic problems, listened to his adenoidal struggle to spell and read, and tried to help him see the difference between a noun and a verb. But alas, neither Mrs. Harmell's encouragement nor my callow tutoring was enough to save Clayton from the awful specter of eighth-grade exams. Back in those days the state of Idaho required every student to pass an examination before receiving an eighth-grade diploma.

Then came the day of the test, administered by Miss Etta VanEtten, county superintendent of schools. All the eighth-grade students from the four one-room schools scattered the length of Little Lost Valley came together in the hamlet of Howe for the ordeal. There were nine of us, as I recall. The first half of the test was arithmetic and English. The second half was Idaho history. We knew if we didn't pass the test we could still go through the graduation ritual planned for the following week in the dance hall of the Howe saloon—except those who failed would receive a diploma that was not signed. We were all practically insensate with worry, which is hardly the proper frame of mind in which to take a test. But poor Clayton was mentally paralyzed. What few fragments of information we had been able to pound into his unformed mind deserted him long before we all sat down at a desk with sharpened pencils and erasers laid neatly before us.

"Sit in front o' me," he whispered to me frantically, as though I were his only hope. Only after I sat down did I understand his strategy. "If ye'll scooch over to one side, I kin see yer answers," he muttered in my ear.

But Miss Etta VanEtten, who had trod the board floors of many country schoolhouses giving such tests and who seemed to have a nose for ferreting out possible malfeasance, placed an empty seat between Clayton and me. No matter how far I scooched over, Clayton wouldn't be able to see my answers, for he was horribly nearsighted.

I was both relieved and regretful. Would I have helped Clayton? Probably. I remember a school superintendent saying to me years later when I was teaching school, "Someone's got to help these kids." He meant the Claytons who enter the world three steps behind everyone else and keep falling back from there on. He was a man who believed every student was worthy of extra help, until the student proved he or she wasn't. I think I would have helped Clayton if I could have.

"Take your pencils," crackled Miss Etta VanEtten in a voice that sounded like it had been raised from a dust bin. "Do not begin until I say 'go.' And please attend to your own work."

There it was. I didn't know it at the time, but she was telling me something I was not going to forget. There are some things in this world no one can do for you. Everyone has to do his own attending.

Clayton did not attend. It was beyond him. He received an unsigned diploma, and there ended his public education. Two years later, when he turned eighteen, he soundly thrashed Old Man Hall and left the valley to enlist in the army. Clayton never came back. On an island somewhere in the Pacific he laid down the life that he had tried briefly and rather unsuccessfully to live. His accomplishments were few, but they don't look quite so pathetic when viewed in the light of the paltry advantages he was offered.

I'm not like the mystics who piously affirm that life is always good if we will only attend to it. I look at the Claytons and wonder what God is up to sometimes. What is real? What is illusion? What of the incompetents, the abstruse, the sinned against, the ones who were not created equal, who never had a chance? I've listened to various explanations but never felt totally satisfied with any of them.

Maybe Annie Dillard was right when she said, in her own peculiar imagery, "We're logrolling on a falling world, of time released from meaning and rolling loose, like one of Atlanta's golden apples, a bauble flung and forgotten, lapsed, and the gods on the lam."[1] And maybe it was because somewhere along the way too many people told God, as they would tell a naughty child, to shut up and go to his room. We asked God not to speak, and God answered our prayer by being silent. Now, perhaps, the only way we can hear the voice of God is to learn to listen to the silence, to attend, to center, and there perhaps to undergo the dread dark night of the soul, so that we can light candles and offer prayers of penance for the mistreatment of all the Claytons of the world, seeking a workable compromise between the absurdities of existence and the holiness of life.

Me? I'll keep dancing until I get to the center, until I find the eye of the storm, the middle of the pond where the stone was tossed that caused the ripples of pain in the first place. I don't know any better way. "Dwell in me, as I in you." I let the words repeat themselves over and over, until saturated with their cadence and imagery, I finally begin to live them.

I remember one particular stormy night, waking suddenly, wondering if the cat wanted in. I stood on the patio and looked out. Nothing but the heavy sound of rain running off the roof, spilling over the gutters, churning the stream below the house into a minor torrent. No stars visible, not even any tiny points of light on the island across the bay. The cat came running toward me from under the protection of a bush, his paws matted with mud, his glossy coat streaking rainwater. With happy mewings he bounded into my arms and snuggled down against my robe. He looked back at the rainy night from which he had emerged, ears lifted, wondering if he should really give it up after all. He seemed almost content to surrender the night prowl, but not totally. I stood for a moment, sensing the indecision in the wet, furry body pressed against me, feeling the racing heartbeat and hearing the rumbling purr. I turned and carried him inside out of the storm.

How many times, I wonder, have I not run to God in just such a manner, weary and blemished from trying to force life to a mold that my will had shaped instead of allowing life to flow through me. Even as I reached for the embrace of God, there was conflict, indecision, a longing to be here and to be there at the same time. Yet at base, there is no contradiction in those longings, for they are finally harmonized and fused into one longing: a longing God who has been anxiously looking and waiting for me to come home. And in that welcoming embrace, a lifetime of babbled prayers cannot begin to express the gratitude that fills my heart.

A Prayer of Attending

Living–dying, changing–becoming, these are the places where I dwell in you, O God. Help me to attend carefully and prayerfully to my own life, that others may see in me that same truth and compassion that I have seen in Jesus Christ. In confidence and expectation I now wait upon you to reveal your great trust in me. Send me forth as a witness and an attender of the ultimate trust. Graciously, silently, you offer your trust to me. Awkwardly yet gratefully, I receive it. Amen.

Spiritual Exercises
for
Attending

1. Find a place where you can be alone. Sit or lie comfortably and silently intone these words, almost as if you are repeating a mantra, "I am giving my full and complete attention to you, God." After chanting the line for several minutes, remain in the attitude of listening. Imagine your soul standing on tiptoe to hear the One that is closer to you than hands or feet, nearer to you than breathing. What is God saying to you? How are you receiving the message? Write about your experience and response in your spiritual journal.

2. This is a walking meditation. Find a place, either outside or inside, where you can walk unencumbered and unhindered. Contemplate what it means to put one foot in front of another. Attend to your walking. A walking meditation from the Buddhist tradition suggests walking as though stepping on the heads of all beings—not heavily or gingerly but with compassion and loving care. As your feet are lifted and touch the floor, let the act become a blessing to everything and everyone that is figuratively touched by your feet. Attend to each step as a treasure. Then write in your journal about your experience. What difficulties did you encounter? Were you able to overcome them? Who was touched or blessed by your steps? What feelings arose in you?

3. Sit comfortably and breathe naturally. Do not force anything, but attend to your breathing. In Zen fashion, count your breaths up to ten; inhale on one, exhale on two, and so on. When you reach ten, start over. Breathe like this for ten minutes or more. Your breath, which is the most intimate part of your being, is now uniting with the pulse of life that is animated throughout the universe. This is true attending. Record the nuances of your experience in your spiritual journal.

11

Confessing

Blessed are those who confess *their pain and brokenness, for they shall take hold of their healing.*

The contemplative lifestyle calls us to travel simply and lightly. Jesus sent his disciples forth on their first mission of preaching and healing with these instructions:

> *Take nothing for your journey, no staff, nor bag, nor bread, nor money, and do not have two tunics. And whatever house you enter, stay there and from there depart. And wherever they do receive you, when you leave that town shake the dust from your feet as a testimony against them.* (Luke 9:1–5)

He tells these would-be followers to carry little and to journey as though they were only the fluttering awareness of a truth lived somewhere between the mysteries of life and death. He warns them to avoid binding attachments and to eschew common tendencies to judge and condemn.

To journey lightly across this earth has to do with more than our outward manner of dress, what we eat, where we live, or adopting a lifestyle, which in time will itself become another weight to shed. To journey lightly requires the daily practice of confession, something few of us are prone to do with regularity. Through confession we throw off the burden of our sins and the strangling load of our attachments in order to receive the new life.

As I began work on this chapter, I engaged a good friend in dialogue on the subject. Because of an uncomfortable feeling that rises up in me every time I hear the word *confession*, I wanted a safe place to discuss my antipathy and possibly my heresies. Because I knew my searching hunger was parallel in many ways with this friend's, I knew I could trust the source. The conversation began with my espousing the conventional mode:

HE: *You know, this whole matter of confession seems to be largely overlooked in the new swing that spiritual formation seems to be taking these days.*

SHE: *Thank God for that.*

HE: *What do you mean? Confession is an inseparable part of our Christian tradition.*

SHE: *That doesn't make it right. What little I know about God (not think but actually am certain about)* *assures me that the standard-brand confessing of sin in order to be forgiven is utter nonsense—or worse, blasphemy. I always choke on prayers of confession in church.*

HE: *But how else can we respond to God's act of forgiveness and reconciliation in Jesus Christ unless we confess our sins with our whole being? Isn't confession the way we receive God's forgiveness?*

SHE: *I don't believe that God has a storehouse of forgiveness, stockpiled somewhere, which is dispensed only after the penitent recognizes sin, grovels a bit, and asks for forgiveness. One of the few things I am sure of is that forgiveness is the very nature of God. It is not a gift that can be withheld or given. Why, the parable of the Prodigal Son ought to teach us that if nothing more.*

HE: *Yet the fact is that we humans, like the son in that parable, are weak and failing creatures, separated from God by our innate selfishness and daily in need of forgiveness for our wrongdoings and shortcomings.*

SHE: *Of course. I don't deny the need for repentance. The prodigal son had to turn from his self-seeking before he could return to the father. But our shortfalls and wrongdoings are to God what an infant's temper tantrums are to a loving parent. God understands completely and knows that the time is coming when we'll grow up and not have temper tantrums anymore. The loving parent neither punishes nor withholds love but is steadily there, providing stability, acceptance, love.*

What parent would demand, "Now, son, before you can come back into fellowship with me, you must say you're sorry and ask my forgiveness"? If you remember the parable, the prodigal son was not even allowed to recite his carefully rehearsed speech. He was instantly welcomed home, just by the fact he was there.

HE: *If I am hearing you right, you are saying that confession is just placing ourselves before God. Are you inferring we don't need prayers of confessing?*

SHE: *No, I am saying we need to redefine confession. We have to let go of our tantrums in order to be aware once again of intimacy and reconciliation. We have to "arise and go to the Father" before we can be aware again of the Presence. But the turning is within us. It has nothing to do with God forgiving. It has to do with our knowing that God is forgiveness itself. And that, my friend, is the highest I know at this moment.*

The conversation was both unsettling and liberating. It is hard to fly in the face of tradition, knowing that ecclesiastical fingers will be wagging at you as you do. But it is also freeing to realize there are no formulae to be followed on the path to spiritual maturity. All that is required is a letting go of the past and an openhearted seeking of a better future.

Confession is a necessary part of spiritual formation, but it must be more than wallowing in a recital of our sins. After a while, if we are not careful, we begin to take a perverse pleasure in recounting how awful we are. The contemplative lifestyle is more than a call to contemplate our sins. It is a call to contemplate who we really are—holy sons and daughters of a living loving God. It is a call to confess our true identity.

Perhaps a better word for confessing is *owning*. Owning is not just admitting our mistakes. Owning is also claiming the spiritual aspect of our nature and bringing to life the imperishable part of our being that we have allowed to languish and starve from neglect.

We are all binders and collectors of things. We bind ourselves to ideas, experiences, persons, desires, sins, faults and even blessings. In this way we become earthbound, unable to find our way because we are so heavily weighted with our collections. Confession is a part of releasing, or leave-taking, that I spoke of earlier. We should not think we do this once and then never have to do it again. We will need to do it daily, in order to separate ourselves from inordinate attachments and to be free to travel lightly. The spiritual journey takes a lifetime, and it will demand of us a condition of complete simplicity, total honesty, costing us everything.

A kind of naive reinvention of religion seems to be going on in our world today. This is partly the outgrowth of rejecting conventional religion as fear-oriented and guilt-producing. It is true that conventional religion has fixed itself doggedly on the negatives, which is partially why it has not succeeded in transforming human society more totally. We should reject any religion that is fear-oriented. But some of these modern substitutes also need careful evaluation. It is hard to describe them in a single word. Some assume the shape of cults under the dominion of guru. Some fly under the banner of "New Age," as though everything that went on in the past should be abandoned. Others offer alternative systems of thought and behavior that encourage people to believe that thanks to their acquisition of a higher order of thinking, they are entitled to exploit others without feeling guilty. And some are predicated on systems of instant enlightenment, painless transformation or boundless prosperity schemes.

Christianity and the great monotheistic religions were not built on a consoling or selfish vision of the nature of existence but rather from a demand made on men and women to become more than they naturally want to be, to transcend themselves through the disciplines of prayer and sacrifice, to be in this world to give and not to take, to love and not to hate. Some of the new forms of religion talk little, if at all, about such disciplines as confessing or owning. Theirs is more a way to feel good without being good, to have it all without giving anything, to vibrate with the rhythms of the universe without any cost to the ego.

Soul-building, which is what we should all be about in this age or any age, like any other natural process, is gradual and painfully slow. What begins in us as a vague uneasiness about our own life and a growing disaffection with the culture in which we live, slowly becomes a serious desire to reexamine the road we are traveling as well as to explore the persons we are. We begin to call into question many of the assumptions on which we have built our lives. We look about us and realize the outer world has become glittering, pompous and vacant for us in many ways. It is at that point we begin to look for something more. Our exploration directs us to look within, and somewhere we cross a mysterious border into the spiritual world, never to turn back.

Spirituality, which is the art of seeking union with God, is really the art of soul-building. We begin the work of fashioning our souls, our true lives, even though we know it will be the work of the rest of our years and that it will be made up of endless and trivial repetitions of such practices as confession. Now and then we will rise to magnificent heights and live on the peaks, but for the most part we must find our way through a maze of valleys, dealing with the little times and small events that make up most of life. Even the terrible threat of nuclear annihilation must be seen as a small problem in light of the greater challenge of soul-building. Otherwise, we will never solve the nuclear problem.

Soul-building does not call for extravagant demonstrations of faith. We don't need to seek supernatural manifestations or perform miraculous acts. What we need is to walk with patient perseverance and steadiness through the humdrum and the monotonous, as well as through the dangerous and the fearful, to the place of our true being.

The new wilderness of our present time must be faced with the same quiet declaration of a Martin Luther, who stood before the Diet at Worms and avowed, "Here I stand, I can do no other." So we stand with patient commitment before the onslaught of a thousand ordinary moments and ordinary people, as well as the threat of annihilation or extinction. We are, as Howard Thurman suggested, keeping a troubled vigil at the bedside of the world. This vigil demands a calm abiding of the issue, a quiet and self-possessed waiting for something, an expectation that refuses to be diminished by discontent or rage or madness.

Soul-building requires that we be gentle with ourselves, in order to be gentle with our world. We should not belabor our sins nor force ourselves to go against the grain of who we truly are. But we must confess both our sins and our true being. We must let grace meet us where we are and play freely with the ordinary daily-ness of our lives, so that in time grace can begin to build the true self out of what we uniquely have been given.

Through dogged patience and persistent confession, we will gain at long last our original face.

Confession did not enter my life until I was fifteen years old. I knew what it was to do wrong and to feel sorry for it, usually because of getting caught. But I didn't know how to apprehend grace and forgiveness in a spiritual way. I wasn't even aware there were such things.

My experience of confession came about when I went to a revival service in the little Baptist church in Arco, Idaho, where I was living with my grandparents while attending high school. The religious background of my family was varied, running from the Mormonism of my father to the Episcopalianism of my grandmother, with many blank spots in between. I always knew there was a God. I would even talk to God on occasion, and sometimes I would confess my sins and ask to be made better. I also prayed if life became too heavy and burdensome, but for the most part I took prayer about as seriously as I took shaving. I knew there would come a time when I would have to do it. Until then, I was content to wait.

Then some kind of momentum came into my life and propelled me to visit the little lava-rock Baptist church one cold January night, 1946, when most folks were home by their fires listening to the "Lux Radio Theater" or "Fibber McGee and Molly." An evangelist had been imported by the Baptists to save that predominantly Mormon community and anyone else who was endangered from "going to hell in a handbasket," which is how my grandfather described it. I was not quite sure what he meant, but I was sure one ought to avoid it if possible. However, I probably would not have gone to church that night had not the local minister arranged for the visiting evangelist to speak at an assembly of the high school student body.

There we sat that afternoon, a group of some seventy souls, and in the mind of the evangelist, I am sure, all seventy of us probably unsaved. The students in Arco High School were drawn from farms and ranches throughout Butte County, as well as the town itself. Bill Bowers smelled like cow manure because he had been wading in the stuff in the cold hours of dawn. Clara Jensen, a nice Mormon girl, had a big hole in the back of her stocking. And Marie Stauffer was sporting a reddish blue hickey on her neck, probably placed there the night before by Garth Purvis. But we lined ourselves up obediently to hear the visiting preacher—cow manure, torn stocking, hickey and all—because hearing a preacher couldn't be any worse than studying algebra.

It was a good deal better, at least for me. I rather liked the evangelist, and I didn't much like algebra. He was pleasant in appearance and warm in manner. He didn't labor to impress or convince. He just talked simply and earnestly about the importance of loving God and letting God love us. He read some verses from the Bible and explained who Jesus Christ was and what he had come here to do. Such a sectarian assembly would probably be forbidden in the halls of public learning today. Fortunately it was allowed then or I might have missed one of the most important decisions of my life, which was to go to church that night to hear him again.

What a difference a setting makes. In the high school assembly, the preacher was personable and friendly. Behind the pulpit, however, he became stern, domineering and uncompromising. He talked about hell, and each time he spoke that word he added a syllable, until "hay-ai-ai-l" reverberated ominously through that lath and plaster sanctuary. Having finally described hell and the various routes you take to get there, he began to lay out what you can do to avoid it. At that point I began to get suspicious in the same way I get suspicious today when I flip on the television and see a telephone number at the bottom of the screen. Something was going to be asked of us before we got out of there, especially those of us who weren't too sure of our eternal destination.

I was right. During the singing of a hymn ("Just As I Am," what else?) he interrupted each verse and told us to get down to the front of the church as fast as we could and confess our sins. Had I been of a mind to confess mine, I wouldn't have chosen that place to do it. But I was uncomfortable ("under conviction," they told me later) and vowed that when I got out of that place I would not soon be returning.

The hymn was over, only to be repeated. The evangelist now was not just pleading, he was threatening. O God, get this over with, I begged silently. Then something inside of me shifted. I don't know exactly what it was nor do I know why, but years later I would be able to look back at that moment and clearly know, "Here I was turned." I saw Jesus before me, arms opened wide, inviting me to step away from the pain and wilderness of my life. The divorce of my parents, my mother's marriage to a man who seldom looked at me or spoke to me, the loneliness and shyness that often threatened to overwhelm—all rose up before me as misplaced pieces in the puzzle of my life and then fell into place somehow. With absolutely no motivation but need, a need held up in humility and simplicity of heart, I stepped out into the aisle. I was again the little boy, too young to read, who would go to my mother, book open in my hands, eager to have her read me a story. In the same childlike way, I opened my life and offered it to God without words and without conditions.

Somewhere in the poetry that haunts my memory is a line about the special place God has for stillborn things, "those things that never were but should have been." I have searched in vain for the full verse and its author, but can only remember these few lines, perhaps not accurately:

God treats them very tenderly for He Knows
what the pain of stifled things can be.

I was a stillborn, a stifled thing, making my way down the aisle that night. But for a few miraculous moments my heart sang, and a flame that had been trying valiantly to burn in my heart suddenly blazed forth with passion. I was found. I was alive. I was Home.

As the evangelist took my hand, when I arrived at the front of the church, his first words to me were prepotent and prophetic, "God bless you, son. You'll never regret what you've done tonight." I never have. It was the singularly most important decision of my life. His next words to me were somewhat spoliating, a mutilation of that tender connectedness I was experiencing. "Now, why don't you kneel down here and confess your sins?"

I don't know where I found the courage to say it, but I answered him, "That's already been done." It had. Even if I had not used the right words, or any words, I had an overriding sense of having been forgiven.

What did I do? As far as I know, nothing but let things happen. It was action through nonaction, letting go of oneself. Nothing could be simpler. Yet consciousness forever interferes when we try to step out of our own way—negating, correcting, editing, selecting—until the simple act of letting go becomes one of the most difficult endeavors of all.

Does this mean we can reject the regularity of prayer and rely on the inspiration of the heart, only confess when we are touched by the spirit? No. The routing of confession breeds attention, calling forth a response of the soul that would otherwise lie dormant. I may never again have a moment exactly like that one in the church aisle, but I cannot live basking only in the reflection of its rays. I must continually pray for forgiveness and for a meeting of the Spirit, if I am truly committed to a life of holiness. Otherwise, I will live only at the threshold and never have an opportunity to cross over into that mysterious realm where God delivers me from myself and takes the matter out of my hands for a little while.

Confession, if sincerely observed, will eventually take us to that point in life where we will yearn for something more spiritual than what we have. There will grow an inner conviction that we are made for much more than anything we have yet known. We know the wonder and power of our bodies, but we also have confronted their limitation and frailty. We likewise have begun to recognize that our minds will take us only so far and that our emotions seem to follow cycles that lead us either to brief euphoria or empty exhaustion. What is this hunger that will not be satisfied, this yearning that will not be stilled? I think it is what the mystics call divine discontent. We have lived the two-dimensional life of body and mind to their limits, and we know there must be something more.

Contemporary Western religion tells us to be satisfied with what we have, for it is not comfortable with pathways that extend beyond body and mind. How odd that religion along with culture should focus only on the well-being of the body and mind and neglect that third dimension, the spirit. How especially odd that Christianity should do this, when biblical tradition seems to indicate quite the opposite. Beyond body ("soma") and mind ("psyche") was stressed spirit ("pneuma"), meaning wind, breath, spirit, oneness. There is a way, said Jesus, that follows the way of the wind, which blows wherever it will. It is a way beyond sense, feeling and thought. It is a way of grace that seeks humility, openness and simplicity. It is the way of the spirit, the way of confession.

Many Christians grow defensive when you suggest to them they are only giving lip service to spirit. Yet observe how uncomfortable most of us are with silence, with stillness, with listening. Observe how successfully even the experience of "speaking in tongues" seeks to negotiate the ebb and flow of emotions and physical feelings, how it limits itself to the first two dimensions. Even where there is talk of "living in the Spirit," there is an assumption that we are destined only for the two-dimensional life of the body and mind.

So we are filled, but we do not see. We are taught, but we do not hear. We go on looking for our true lives, for the ever-elusive abundant life, for God, but we never seem to find them. We look "out there," in securely marked-off sanctuaries and in physical or mental manifestations that we try to disguise as experiences of the spirit. But somehow we do not connect.

The result is a growing sense of spiritual discontent. We tend to keep our disturbing questions to ourselves and to go on pretending that we are participating with God in the venture of life. But the truth is that most of the time we are not sure about anything, especially God.

When we are honest enough to own our need, to confess our desperate hunger, the road to the spirit will be opened before us. It is not a well-charted road, but we have the guidance of many great souls who have walked it before us, and we have a Soul Guide in Jesus Christ. To follow him is to set out on the ways that penetrate beyond mind and body toward our own Godwardness and the true goal of our life.

Pay no attention to those who tell you that looking for God within is wrong. Do not even hear them. A long and sacred tradition, built on biblical precepts, would have you know that the eternal Word of God lies hidden in each of us, waiting to generate the life of heaven in our souls. Though God is everywhere present, God is not present to you unless found in the deepest and most central part of your soul. "Christ in you," said the Apostle Paul, "the hope of glory."

If we reach for God through our faculties of understanding, will and memory, we will never possess God or be united to God. Only as we begin to search and dig in the field of our own being can we discover the hidden treasure that poor Isaac traveled so far to find. Within that infinite part of our own being rests the infinity of God. God has made each of us for Godself, and what we are to God is what we really are. If our lives are hid with Christ in God, as scriptures affirm, then there is an inner grace ceaselessly at work within us, tirelessly calling us to turn ourselves to God, to confess our true being.

The divinely ordained plan that God has for each of us is always being revealed to us, if we have the eyes and ears to apprehend. Through daily experiences, innumerable encounters with persons and situations, through successes and failures, we are slowly being awakened to that plan and to the realization that God's providence is always operating on our behalf, not outside but within our own spirit. We may not see it at the time, but later we will look back and mark the fact that at each state of life the plan was being revealed and unfolded. Cooperating with the plan is letting ourselves be created.

Writer and mystic Jean-Pierre de Caussade has said that we must allow each moment to be the cause of the next, the reason for what precedes being revealed in what follows, so that everything is firmly and solidly linked together in a divine chain of events. Observing my own life, I have seen this occurring. The way has always opened up before me as I walked. Even if I moved forward with a sense of helplessness, it later became clear that God was close beside me at each step and in all the various situations that arose.

After my momentous decision to be publicly and formally yoked to Christ and following this with baptism, it would have been nice to think the plan was all laid out and no more choices would be necessary. But the task of having to make choices is never-ending; it was still before me, even more sharply. I had now become aware of the necessity of good and wise choices if my life was to be true to the experience of the reality of God that I had had in the church aisle. That experience had kindled a light in me that could not be quenched, and I earnestly desired to make my choices based on a loyalty to the response of that moment, that my faith might be sustained and deepened. To that end I selected Linfield College, a Baptist-related school in Oregon, as the setting for the next chapter of my life.

It was a strange and frightening venture for me to go so far away from home. I had never been out of the state of Idaho, except for a few trips to Utah to meet my father's people. No one from my family had ever gone to college. I was moving out on my own into an unknown world. I am sure I could not have done it if there had not been that lifting of the veil at the horizon of the unknown when I glimpsed a vision of the eternal. I wanted to be devoted to God. I wanted to do what was expected of me. I longed to be faithful. So I chose Linfield College, and with a modest scholarship and a limited savings of wages earned by working in a grocery store after school and on Saturdays, I made my preparations to leave home.

Someone has said that the miracle is just to walk the earth. To me the miracle is that I ever walked away from home. I loved my mother dearly, and I was not particularly brave or adventuresome. Why then did I do it? Part of it may have been that home in the house of my stepfather was an uncertain place for me. I knew there were no more benefits for me there, that after high school graduation I was expected to be on my own. Another part of my decision was that I did not want to spend my life clerking in a small-town grocery store or working on a ranch, both worthy professions but not what I wanted. But the major factor was that I had come to accept my life as a unique drama of revelatory events, and I felt God calling me to lean into divine will for my vocation. The beginning step toward that vocation was college.

I had no idea to what profession I was being called. I thought of teaching, journalism, social work. I did not think of ministry. My head was straining to see the whole way, complaining that I did not have enough money for even the first step in this venture. But my heart was content with that one step. There is in each of us a way of living that has to do with the courage to trust the ultimate knowing of the heart. This, I was to discover, is the province of true religion. So I took the end of the golden thread, which William Blake said leads us in at heaven's gate, and made my way to college.

On the night before I was to leave, my mind anxious with many projected images and concerns, the Baptist pastor came to see me. He asked if I would go for a drive with him. I was impatient with this interruption, but knowing the sincere and good intentions of this man, I went along.

Twilight was descending as we drove Arco's main street. We then crossed the Lost River that watered the length of the valley, passed through open fields that were fragrant with the scent of freshly cut alfalfa, and parked on a bluff looking back at the twinkling lights of the hamlet that nestled itself between the edge of the desert and the rise of the mountains. We had talked about inconsequential things as we drove, and all the while I was secretly wondering what he was up to. Now as we sat there, looking at the town and valley that had always been my home and that soon I would leave, he began to speak.

"Rodney, I wanted a chance to pray with you before you leave. I wanted a chance to tell you that I feel your life is destined to count in some significant way for God's work, perhaps in the ministry, and that I hope you will always keep close to God. You are going into a new situation, where everyone will be a stranger. Let God be your friend, and never hesitate to talk to him when you need to, and to trust him to complete in you the work he has begun. You have many gifts that would be a great blessing to others. I hope you will always offer those gifts to God." With that he prayed for me, asking God to bless me and to go with me.

It was a silent drive home. I was slightly embarrassed, I must confess. Such overt religious expression was still new to me, and I had no clear idea what prayer could do for me in this life adventure. As to the notion of my having special gifts, I was at that time so shy and insecure within myself that I had trouble believing I could be much of a success at anything important.

Some moments remain in our memories to light up our minds with a kind of transcendent glory. It happens to all of us. We can look back and find such times, sharp and clear in detail, and perhaps not know why they remain with such distinction and radiance. Yet we know that whenever they flash back from the past the whole world seems to glow inside our being. Perhaps these are the moments that signal us to the fact that a sacred reality lies within us that transcends all the ordinary moments of our human existence. So that evening, when a pastor prayed for my future, stands as singular, augural, holy, as a time when I began to believe a little more in myself.

I have always had a wish to know the future, especially when I stand on the threshold of any new adventure. I wanted to know when I left home for college that all would be well, that I would be modestly successful and find the peace that belongs to the contented. But the future is not ours to know. I had to learn then, what I have had many occasions to remember, that the future is only made meaningful by the past. All that we have learned, felt and thought, all the love that has nourished us, all those who have cared for us—all these and more are with us as we move into the unknown. And always there is the One who invites us to take the road and who walks with us as we journey. "He leads us on paths we do not know," my friend and mentor Howard Thurman used to say. Indeed, God does just that. But in the course of our journey through this wilderness, we need to learn a rhythm of understanding when to lead and when to follow.

Can we begin to realize the true depth that lies just below the surface of our daily circumstances? Can we begin to see every moment as sacramental and every soul as precious? Can we find the strength now and then to take our own life into our arms and kiss it, scars and all? That's part of confessing, seeing the worth and the holiness in ourselves, in everything.

What have I suggested thus far? I am suggesting that as we remember, we will begin to release our pain and take hold of our healing. As we treasure, we will accept the miracle that we are. As we attend, we will come to learn the techniques of focusing clearly and quietly, of being fully present to life and God in it. As we confess, we will come to accept our actions, indeed our very lives, and trust the disclosures they bring. And our experience of all that, down to the very moment of my writing this page and your reading it, is the uncovering of a part of the gentle winds that forever blow us to the shores of the unexpected islands.

A Prayer of Confessing

Sometimes, O God, your word is too much for me. You ask me to love my enemies, when I can scarcely love my friends as I should. You ask me to give when I want to take. You ask me to forgive when I want to nurse my bitterness. I confess my failings and ask to be freed of the burden of regret and self-recrimination. I also confess who I really am: your holy child, created by love, to live in love, for the sake of love. Free me from my procrastinations and help me do what you have told me. Teach me your compassion that I might not hurt others thoughtlessly, but instead bring light and hope to them. Help me to know your truth that I might be free in your love. Amen.

Spiritual Exercises
for
Confessing

1. In your journal quickly write answers to the following questions. Who am I? What have I come here to do? Am I doing it? How could I be doing it better? Write your first, unedited responses.

2. Sit quietly, entering a still, meditative state, and imagine yourself on a witness stand. You are being asked to tell the truth and nothing but the truth. You are being told to confess every mean and shameful deed you have ever committed. As you begin your confession, in your mind's eye see those you have wronged. Admit your thoughtlessness and wrongdoings. Be truthful but also be gentle with yourself. Let the heavy energy of your past mistakes drain away from your center, being released in the act of confession. With each confession, repeat the words, "I am forgiven, I am restored, I am renewed. Grace replaces guilt." When you have finished your confession, rise from the witness stand and step down. Notice there is no judge and no jury. Only you convict yourself, and only you, through your heartfelt confession before God, can absolve yourself.

3. Take a walk in a place where, if possible, you will not meet anyone. Imagine that an unseen companion is walking beside you, arm in arm. You feel very comfortable with the presence

of this companion. Now your companion begins to speak to you, praising you for many unique attributes, for the radiant facets of your physical, emotional and spiritual selves. Accept the praise with an open heart. Let it flow to the center of your being. Slowly, surely, by the end of your walk, you will have glimpsed, at long last, your true and original self.

4. After completing the above exercises, review what you wrote in your journal in exercise 1, above. Do you have any new responses to the questions, Who am I? What have I come here to do? Am I doing It? How could I be doing it better? Have exercises 2 and 3, above, freed you to a new sense of worth and self-esteem? By this comparison, you may learn the value of freeing yourself through confession.

12

Connecting

Blessed are those who connect to all things
and refuse all sense of separation,
for they shall become one with God.

I pull a box of yellowed newspaper clippings from the top shelf of a closet. I open it and feel that I am opening myself, looking again at the pain and the happiness of being created, reshaped, expanded. Why did I save them? After all these years, what meanings can these storied words convey?

HIGH SCHOOL GRADUATES TWELVE. It was May 1947. I was the class salutatorian. My speech: "Faith and Life." A presumptuous topic for a sixteen-year-old who was graduating two years ahead of schedule because of starting the first grade at the age of five and blending seventh and eighth grades into one year. Yet there I was holding forth on "Faith and Life," as though I knew something about both, as though I were already the theologian, the philosopher.

LOCAL COUPLE MARRIED IN HOME CEREMONY. The wedding of Cleo and Dee. I was part of the wedding party. Some might consider that ironic, since I had casually dated Cleo in my early high school years; had, that is, until religion pulled me over to one side and directed me to look seriously at such dangers as being "unequally yoked." Cleo was a Mormon; I was a Baptist.

TAYLORS CELEBRATE FIFTIETH. From the brittle journalistic heirlooms, I lift out the faces of my grandmother and grandfather, smiling behind a three-tiered cake that denotes their fiftieth wedding anniversary. Married February 21, 1899. Now I am reading that on February 20, 1949, the Arco Recreation Hall was packed with friends from the length and breadth of Lost River Valley, who had come to salute these much-loved pioneer residents. On the program was one of the grandsons, who had been the recipient of the generous love of John and Margaret Taylor: "Rodney Romney, accompanied by Emmabelle Ellingford, sang, 'When Your Hair Has Turned to Silver.'" A normal singing voice, moderately true, but never destined to set the musical world on its ear. I wonder where he ever found the courage to overcome his demons of timidity enough to render such an offering.

Attached to that clipping emerged another announcing the death of Mrs. John Taylor. Death entered our family for the first time in my experience. The grandmother who had always been there for us, who was the mainstay of our family, drawing us together for celebrations and reestablishment of our connections of origin, was dead. She would be followed a year and a half later by my grandfather.

From the box I draw out another clipping, dated May 26, 1949, three months after the celebration of my grandparents' anniversary. This one dances before my eyes, creating a momentary disorientation as the grip of the subconscious begins to fill in the details of the ready-made memory evoked by the headline: GIRL, 16, DIES IN STANLEY AUTO MISHAP.

How natural to let that faded newsprint propel me backward through time until I locate myself in the tragedy of that event and ask the poet's question, "Where is the life we have lost in living?" This question must be answered but not in ways that will plunge us into more of life or into an automatism of experience, nor even into a melancholic examination of the past. If we are going to learn life, we may have to unlearn many of the patterns and ways to which we have adapted ourselves. We may have to release the imprisoned self that lies beneath the layer of past events and conditioning, until we experience that timeless moment where the succession of time is an abstraction rather than a reality and where the real state of the universe is perceived as eternal, without past or future. We must dwell in the secret parts of our being, until one day we are able to live through questions and separations and emerge into the great principle of universal connectedness.

"In thy sight a thousand years are but as yesterday, that has come and gone" sang the psalmist (Psalm 90:4, Knox Version). Time doesn't pass any faster for God than it does for us. In fact, for God there is no passing of time. All the eons become one timeless moment. So when we connect to God, we move out of *chronos* time, the passing of moments where life is lived anticipating the future, and into *kairos* time, not linear time at all, but the kind of time the Gospel talks about as fulfillment: "In the fullness of time, God sent forth his son." "When his time had fully come, he went forth." In that mysterious merging of the unique with the universal into a sense of season due, the transformation of *chronos* into *kairos* takes place. Eternity invades our mortality, and we arrive at connectedness.

But who was the "girl, 16" of the headline? She was Patricia Ann Lee, who had lived in Stanley, Idaho and had attended high school in nearby Challis. She had a cascade of wavy red hair that picked up the brilliance of sunlight and sent it bouncing in auburn prisms in all directions, a shy smile, gray-green eyes rimmed with auburn lashes, and a generous dusting of tan freckles across her face and arms. None of these features alone distinguished her as beautiful but together they did establish her as intriguing and undeniably striking. She turned heads wherever she walked in her slim lissomeness. I was a little bit in love with her. So was everyone else in Stanley.

What was I doing in Stanley, nearly 200 miles northwest of Arco? I was teaching school. Eighteen years old, one year of college, and I was teaching school. Two factors conspired to make this possible: a drastic shortage of teachers in Idaho and not enough money in my bank account to return to college. "Work a few years, earn some money, then go back and complete your education." That was the standard advice from nearly every quarter, especially from those who felt I might approach them for a loan. The little school in Stanley was open. I could qualify to teach on a provisional certificate. I knew country school punctilios, since I was the product of such a school. It would be good experience and help me decide if teaching was to be my profession.

Stanley, back in those days, was a tiny alpine hamlet with less than fifty permanent residents. It nestles at nearly 7,000 feet against the magnificent backbone of the blue spires of the Sawtooth Mountains and near the headwaters of the Salmon River, designated in legend as the River of No Return. Its pristine, isolated splendor was then and still is breathtaking, although Stanley has now been discovered by the outside world. Much of its rustic, primitive charm has been altered, first by the hippies with their tents and shacks, then by the precursors of the yuppies, who built their palatial summer homes along the river and lakes.

My first year in Stanley was in many ways difficult. I was drawn into some of the valley feuds that trace their origins to early days. I was lonely, especially during the winter months when heavy snows and subzero weather sealed us off from contact with the outside world. I was young and socially immature for the vocational role in which I found myself. But I liked teaching. And I loved that stalwart little army of boys and girls, most of whom traveled many miles each day from the sweep and depth of the basin to the log schoolhouse in Stanley. Among my students were Davy and Bobby Lee, lovable little rascals, each with a thatch of red hair, each with a liberal portion of freckles. These two began a quiet conspiracy of seeing that their older sister Pat and I somehow got together when she came home on weekends.

Pat played the piano. Hers was not a classical genius. It was a honky-tonk style that had adapted itself to local dances. When I first heard her play, I decided we had a few things in common—a good sense of rhythm but a limited mastery of the keyboard in a technical way. We sometimes sat at the old upright piano in the school and talked about chord progressions, modulations and the thing we both did best—improvisations. She taught me the melody to "My Adobe Hacienda," and I taught her the harmonies to "Darktown Strutters' Ball."

There were a number of young people in Stanley that year. The Shaws, who ran the Stanley Garage, provided three: David, Kent and Dorothy, who was Pat's friend and schoolmate. Other young adults, sprinkled up and down the Stanley Basin, periodically gathered for parties, dances and skiing with the Shaws, and I was included in these social shirrings. They helped pass the lonely hours of winter and gave a ripeness to life that I still recall as exalting.

One May evening a group of us met spontaneously at the Shaws. No agenda. School was out for those who were involved in it. I was staying on in Stanley to work at the store and post office for the summer and had signed a contract to teach there another year. David Shaw asked me to ride with him up to Redfish Lake on an errand, after which we would meet the group and drive down to "Torrey's on the River" for an evening of dancing. Pat and I would alternate on the piano, with anyone else who played an instrument welcome to join in. It was great to be young and alive on such a splendid evening with such a congenial group.

David and I drove to Redfish Lake and returned to Stanley as the alpenglow was beginning to settle over the snow-covered peaks of the Sawtooths. We pulled into the Shaw yard to be met by Preston, his father. "Been a bad accident," he announced without preliminaries, his usually friendly face set in grim lines. "Dorothy, Jean and Pat were driving Wayne's car to lower town." (There are two Stanleys, Upper and Lower, the result of an old feud.) "Pat was at the wheel. On the way something went wrong, and they went into the river. Jean and Dorothy are bruised and banged up, but okay. I just brought them here to the house. Pat's hurt bad. She's down on the road. A doctor from Twin Falls, who happened to be going by, is with her. We'll need this car to take her to the hospital in Hailey."

The story was tersely laid out. We sprang into action. Questions could wait. A mattress was brought hastily from the house and stuffed into the back seat of the big sedan we were driving, turning it into a kind of ambulance. We quickly drove the several miles down the winding gravel highway, which snaked itself above the river, until we came to a gathering of people and cars at a place where the road curved. I saw first the 1936 black coupe, lying in the water against a huge rock, about fifty feet from the bank. Its top, poking out above the swirling currents, was bashed in. The skid marks it had made in its fatal plunge down the bank were plainly visible in the early dusk.

Then I saw Pat. She was lying on a pile of jackets and coats at the edge of the road. Her eyes were closed. Her beautiful hair was wet and matted about her deathly pale face. A man was kneeling beside her. As we got out of the car and approached them, the man stood up and shook his head. "She's dead," he announced flatly. "Skull undoubtedly fractured."

There was a moment of stunned silence among that knotted clump of humanity, broken only by the roar of the swollen river. Then Preston Shaw, practical and action-oriented, turned to David and said, "We'll put her in the car and take her to the mortician in Challis."

We tenderly lifted her broken, limp body and placed it on the mattress in the back seat of the sedan. She was now a body, no longer Pat. David and I were chosen to transport her the sixty miles to Challis. We started on our sad and gruesome journey, numb from shock, acutely aware of that silent passenger in the back, and realized that Pat's parents, who had been in Challis for the day, were probably now traveling that same road back to Stanley, unaware that their daughter was dead.

Our headlights cut a yellow swath of light through the lonely darkness, making ghostly shadows out of trees and bushes. We did not talk much at first. I attempted to overcome my inherent timidity about the overpowering presence of death in the car by thinking of other things. But no matter how I tried, I was thrust back again to contemplate how the conditions of despair had brutally collided with the conditions of hope in the lives of all of us in that little community. David gave his attention to negotiating the winding curves. Once he turned and looked in the back seat, something I had studiously avoided doing. He reached over and lightly touched the bare feet that were only inches from my head. "Like ice," he commented. He obviously had had more experience with death than I, for I had been trying to pretend none of this had happened, while he was solidifying the experience by touching it. Manifesting a courage I did not feel, I tentatively brushed my fingers against the flesh that was like frozen marble and felt a coldness go through my soul.

We then began to talk. How could it have happened? What had gone wrong? We knew Pat to be an inexperienced driver. Why had Wayne lent his car to her? More importantly, why had he not gone with her? David had run into the house quickly to see his sister when we stopped there. He said that Dorothy had told him the road was rough as washboards, that the car had been jouncing about, but that their speed was not excessive. She recalled that when the car began to turn toward the river, Pat simply allowed it to move where it would. Even as she and Jean called out to her, Pat sat in a silent trance, staring straight ahead, as she drove over the edge of the thirty-five-foot bank and into the water. Had some mechanism failed in the car? Had something happened to Pat prior to the accident? Had she made some kind of eerie pact with her own death on that evening? We would never know the answers to our questions, but it helped ease the tenseness of the drive to fill the silent spaces with words.

Then in the distance we saw the lights of a car approaching. "Her parents?" I wondered aloud. David admitted he had thought the same thing. I hoped he intended to drive on by if it were and then knew my hope was cowardly. I did not want to be the bearer of the horrible news, a witness to their grief and shock. As the car drew near, David slowed. The other car did the same. In that isolated country, attention is paid to such signals. It might mean help was needed or communication was desired. As we passed, we realized it was indeed Stub and Vella, Pat's parents. Oh, dear God, I thought, let them keep driving. But as we stopped a few feet beyond them, they also stopped.

Stub put his head out the window and called out, "Anything wrong?"

We got out and walked back toward them. I was relying on David, older and more experienced, to carry us through this terrible moment.

"There's been a car accident," said David. "It involved Pat."

Vella was instantly out of the car, moving rapidly in our direction. How Pat resembled her, I thought, as she hurried in our direction. "What's happened?" she demanded. "Is Pat hurt?"

"I'm afraid so," David responded. The maddening way we try to soften the blow, postpone the inevitable. But what other way is better?

"How bad?" Vella's voice was taut, like strings on a guitar stretched to their breaking point.

"Hurt bad," answered David, then a pause. Finally, "I'm sorry to tell you she is dead." He said it gently as you could ever say such words.

Vella stood in the middle of the road as though paralyzed. Stub, who had also gotten out of the car, put an arm around her as he asked, "Where's Pat?" He was struggling to keep his voice steady.

"We have her in the car," said David. "We're taking her to the mortician in Challis."

Vella's heavy cry was like that of a wounded animal, ringing against the rocky walls of the canyon and spreading out over the tops of the pines. Shaking herself loose from Stub, she bounded toward the car and before any of us could stop her had opened the back door and flung herself partway in. She saw the still form on the folded mattress, and from the shock of an anguish that had barely begun to assert itself, she screamed, "Oh, my God, my baby girl! My baby girl!" She stroked the feet. She pulled at the hands. She reached up to touch the face, caress the hair. Her screams dwindled into a crooning moan. "Oh, my baby girl, my baby girl, my baby girl."

We stood back, allowing her that moment. At last Stub tenderly pulled her away. Holding her close against his huge form, he asked us, "How did it happen?"

We told the story as best we could. When we finished, Vella sagged in his arms and groaned, "Oh, God, I don't want to live. I want to die, too."

"Honey, we have our little boys waiting for us at home," said Stub. "We have to go to them now."

I wondered then if anyone had even bothered to tell the boys, if anyone was with them. The realization that someone was depending on her seemed to strengthen Vella. She allowed Stub to lead her to the car. He thanked us, and we separated, they to drive to a home empty of one of its brightest lights, and we to complete our mission of transporting Pat's body to the funeral home.

That night has never left me. It never will. It was to haunt me in many sleepless hours, forcing me to replay every detail and to open myself more fully to the eros of human suffering and pain. The mystics write about the pain that heals. When real tragedy enters the life of a previously unawakened person, bringing darkness where once there was light, the person first passes through intense revolt and shock. But that pain brings with it an unprecedented opportunity to function at a new level of reality, to view the prospect of a transformed life. It may take time for us to allow the transforming process to begin and be completed, but all pain has both the capacity to heal and to bear us up to God.

When the soul had experienced severe suffering, it is like a withered branch, stripped of its growth and vibrancy. But that sere limb is enough for the Holy Spirit to light upon, in the same manner the eagle lights upon the branch of the dead tree to build its nest. And there begins our renewing. God comes and does for us what we cannot do for ourselves. God comes to begin the necessary work of connecting.

We cannot avoid grief and mourning. We should not even try. We may attempt to keep brave for the sake of appearances or to bolster up others, but we are only postponing the day when we must finally admit there is no Garden of Eden, that humanity has fallen heir to a great burden of despair. Yet despair has the mysterious power to achieve in us a fine tempering of personality and a development of our own spiritual resources as we accept it and assimilate it into ourselves.

John Stephenson Rowntree of York once wrote, "There is no sadder thing in life than a wasted sorrow." To utilize sorrow does not require acceptance of the idea that the hardness of this world will be compensated in another. That is scant comfort. Sorrow can be utilized whenever and wherever it comes. I didn't know this when I was eighteen, but today I realize that every tragedy of my life has always offered me great tools if I would first allow myself the right to mourn and then accept the tools that sorrow offers.

I have seen far too many people who stayed present to their pain by anger and bitterness. The result was inevitably ill health, mental breakdown or the shattering of important relationships. We have to let our suffering penetrate into our being, until it ceases to be separate from us and becomes one of our closest associates. Accepting it means forgiving it. And forgiving it means healing it.

Suffering holds within it the potential for tremendous energy. It carries what Pierre Teilhard de Chardin called "the ascensional force of the world." The agony of Christ on the cross is one of the most exalted forms of suffering manifested to our eyes, in which the mysterious and transforming work of creation can be observed. His suffering was a grand act of sublimation and unification that connected him eternally to God and helped the world take a vast leap of connecting to its Creator.

Connecting, joining our lives to eternity, always lies near the place of our emptiness where we are forced to penetrate the mystery that permeates our existence. We follow many visible and outward forms to establish this connectedness, which is at the heart of our deep soul longing. Alan Paton in his writings likened this search to a child's hands reaching for the wild bird, thirsty arms stretched out for water, a woman's waiting in a snowstorm for the long-awaited letter, the savage seeking a tune from the harp, a man raking the ashes of a burned-down house for treasures. We are all searchers, thrusting out our hands for the incomprehensible and the holy, trying to touch the hem of the robe of the Infinite. The visible and outer forms of this search are only symbols of our powerful yearning for the mysterious ground of our being, for the sacred hearth within, where we may find the mystery that worships through us.

Lewis Thomas in his fascinating book, *The Lives of a Cell*, advanced the idea that earth's life is derived from some single cell, fertilized in a bolt of lightning as the earth cooled.[1] Some find such biologic musings a dangerous and blasphemous flirtation with evolution, but I find them strangely reassuring. If we are all progeny of this parent cell, then all life is of one piece, even though the working parts of this earth may seem to lack visible connectedness.

Our destiny then is to establish connections to our origin and to the miracle of a common life that has crossed the abyss between time and eternity and is sharing the earth with us. Death is designed not to be our terror but our hope, our confidence that final connections can be revealed and realized. Death is not merely a biological fact or a psychological loss. Death is a spiritual phenomenon that connects us to eternity.

The philosopher Nietzsche said that the one who has a why to live for can bear with almost any *how*. In other words, why we live enables how we live. If we know that our goal is connecting with eternity, even while struggling in these mortal frames, then we will eventually take responsibility for finding the means for fulfilling that goal.

The preacher from Challis who conducted Pat Lee's funeral said, "Don't ever ask why. It is a useless, futile question." Even as he said those words, I wondered if they really comforted the hearts of Stub and Vella, Davy and Bobby, and the rest of that broken, wondering community. We must have a why, if not to answer our immediate confusions and wonderings, then at least to propel us toward ultimate meanings. Something has to enter and sustain us, or we shall go mad.

Viktor Frankl, writing of his inner attempts to survive the Nazi prison camp, said that he discovered two things that sustained him: the sense he was loved and the challenge of a task. The first came in knowing that his wife loved him devotedly. He found himself connecting with her on more than one occasion. Her presence with him was so strong that he felt he could stretch out his hand and grasp hers. On one occasion, when he was assigned to shovel a trench under the insulting ridicule of guards, he had a strong awareness of her presence, the sense that she was *there*. At that very moment, a bird flew down, perched on the heap of frozen soil that he had dug up from the ditch, and looked steadily at him. The second thing that sustained him was the challenge of a meaningful task. When he was taken to the camp at Auschwitz, a manuscript of his, ready for publication, was confiscated. When he fell ill with typhus, he began to jot down on little bits and scraps of paper his recollections of that writing, from which he believed he would someday be able to reconstruct the manuscript. These two factors, the knowledge he was loved and the challenge of a meaningful task, assisted him in overcoming the danger of collapse. He constructed the why of life from a sense of how and could write triumphantly, "Life ultimately means taking the responsibility to find the right answer to its problems and to fulfill the tasks which it constantly sets for each individual."[2]

Connecting is one of our tasks, and yet it is not dependent on our strength alone. A Power, not our own, stands waiting for us at the pit of every peril, illuminating and transfiguring our adversity and promising an eventual triumph. This is what religion means by faith in God. God can be trusted. God can be relied upon. A table has been prepared in the presence of all our enemies; and though we must drag ourselves to that table, weary foot by weary foot, the Host sent out the invitation long ago and included in it the glad note that the universe is a safe and friendly place and that we would make a safe journey.

Suffering may indeed lure us into the wilderness and not to the banquet table. But there it will speak to us tenderly, as the prophet suggested (Hosea 2:14), helping us to begin the work of connecting to a higher dimension of reality and tranquility. That connecting is not merely vertical. One must not ignore the dynamic of its horizontal aspect. In other words, spirituality is not to be understood as God alive and active in *our* life only. It also is to be understood as God alive in *all* life. Therefore, spiritual growth is anything that creates or enhances our understanding that God is not just an idea or a being "out there somewhere" but a Something or Someone making a difference in our actions and relationships and in the life of the world.

Connecting is not an end in itself. It is the vehicle that allows and encourages us to connect with others and with all creation. Connecting encourages our faithful witness in the world and gives us strength and determination in the struggle for peace and justice for oppressed peoples. Otherwise, religion becomes disconnected. Far too much religion in the world today is moldering in the grave of disconnectedness rather than linked to the world in which it lives.

Let me share the final episode in the Stanley saga and bring this chapter to a close. I have already told you there are two Stanleys, Upper and Lower. That division came about many years ago over a dispute between some early residents, the reasons and details having largely been lost. What remains is the evidence of the feud: two distinct towns, created by one group picking itself up and moving two miles up river, while the other group remained where it was. But though the origins of the feud are hazy, it still has remnants and ramifications. It has so penetrated and imbricated life in that basin that when I was teaching there it was not unusual to find ranchers whose land touched who would not speak to each other because of some minor dispute. One boy told me early in the school year his parents did not want him to play with the children from a certain family because their dads were mad at each other. I told him I would not set him against the rules of his family, but while he was at school under my direction he would have to live by the rules of the school, one being that we were all living, friendly parts of each other.

The death of Patricia Lee presented a new challenge. Her family was poor. Where was the money to pay for a funeral? Someone suggested a community donation, and since I was a neutral person in terms of old factions, that I do it. I was then advised which families not to approach, several of them in Lower Stanley, because of long-standing animosities. Although asking someone for money has never been "my thing," I decided I would do it and that I would give everyone, even those in Lower Stanley, the opportunity to share. The worst they could do would be to say no.

"No" was the answer at the first home I approached. The woman drew herself to stern height and declared sharply, "If I had wanted to do anything for that girl, I would have done it while she was alive. Moreover, I would not lift a finger to help the rest of that family, and if you care to sit down, I will tell you why."

Everyone likes a good story, and maybe on another day I would have listened. That day I did not want to. Begging to be spared her explanations, I made my way to the next house, although with a little less confidence than I had started out with. At that home the husband was present. When I explained why I had come, his wife, standing behind him, began to cry, while he reached for his wallet. "We wuz a-wonderin' how we could help," he mumbled huskily, as he began to dig into his worn leather billfold. "Stub an' me ain't spoke fer years, but I shore am knowin' how tough this must be fer all of 'em."

Their generosity was a foretaste of what I found in every other home I visited. That little community of people, struggling against the odds to survive, dug down deep into their meager resources and contributed over $500 for the Lee family, with only one woman refusing. And at Pat's funeral, those who had held resentments and nourished grudges against each other sat side by side, one in their common bond of grief. At the grave, among the women who embraced Vella was the wife of the husband who had not spoken to Stub for years.

One might say that the good to emerge from Pat's death was the uniting of a community in reconciliation, at least for a moment. Death is always the leveling factor, because it is the universal experience. It may not bring us comfort, but it takes all of us on a journey to truth. It also establishes the bonds of connectedness for which we have always yearned, and it offers us, in the end, the distant view of a transformed life.

At the center of the Christian life is the vibrant yet suffering figure of a man dying on a cross, creatively and lovingly bearing the full weight of the distortion of the world around him. This image is both disturbing and awesome, but in our pleasure-oriented culture, it is a monumental alternative to the superficial happiness we feverishly pursue. That cross is the symbol of reconciliation and connectedness, of God connecting Godself to humanity, of Jesus connecting humanity to God, and of humans connecting to each other in the common gift of grace.

I put the clippings back into the box and close it. The doubt, pain, quandary and loss that they opened in me have become the path to a fuller life. My circle of family and friends is not unbroken, my cherished ambitions and secure foundations of belief are not impregnable, and I am living in the wilderness of an era that sometimes seems to have lost its way. But maybe in the mysterious wisdom of God, this is just the human way. Compassion is not dead, service is still the real path to happiness; peace and justice are more than ideals to be dreamed about, and connecting is the eternal possibility. It is not an easy way to live, but I suspect it is the real way.

A Prayer of Connecting

God of the wilderness, because I dare to believe I am connected to you, I must also believe I am connected to everything you have created. Make true and deep my connections to the one cosmic story that is the story of all. Help my eyes to meet the eyes of others without fear, that we might recognize each other and rejoice in this life that believes in itself and whose highest goal is to connect all of us to our eternal possibilities. So may it be. Amen.

Spiritual Exercises
for
Connecting

1. For those of us who are sighted, we connect most easily to the world through the eyes. The aphorism "The eyes are the windows of the soul" refers to the fact that seeing is the way by which we connect the soul, or the inner, to the outer world. This exercise will offer you the opportunity to make the connection between those two worlds. Sit comfortably where you can have an expansive view of a landscape, seascape, urbanscape, sky—it matters not. Scan the view with your eyes wide open, noting all the visual sensories—color, shape, texture—of the world around you. Then begin consciously to connect your inner self—the eyes of your soul—to everything you see. As you connect inner with outer, repeat the verse "Creation waits with eager longing for the revealing of the sons and daughters of God." Creation hungers for a connection with you. Through confession you have claimed your true nature as a daughter or son of God. Now, as you contemplate the view before you, as you connect at heart and soul level with it, you are sending forth the revelation of love and grace for which creation longs. You are becoming one with all you see, moving from separateness to wholeness, from individual to communal, from one to All. After your contemplations, write your feelings in your journal.

2. The prayer of connecting follows two rhythms: receive and give. The blessings you give out will come back to you, for such is the law of the universe given by Jesus and the prophets. As you move about in the world, quietly affirm this truth, "The measure I give is the measure I will receive." Give love, and you will receive love. Give joy, and you will receive joy. Give yourself, and you will discover the fullness of Self. As you walk the way of connection in your daily life, remember to record your experiences in your spiritual journal. After several weeks, your journal will be the barometer of your unfolding to Spirit and Self.

13

Wrestling

*Blessed are those who wrestle with their own darkness,
for they shall touch again the light from which they came.*

The mysterious story of Jacob wrestling all night with an unnamed divine adversary at Peniel and his subsequent acquiring of the new name of Israel (Genesis 32:22–32) has long haunted religious imagination. Jacob was on his way home to deal with the brother he had betrayed, but first he had to deal with God. In fact, the images of God and Esau, Jacob's brother, are in such careful juxtaposition that they often merge and overlap. The story deserves retelling, not just because of its connections to patricide and sibling rivalry but more importantly because of the theme of God and humanity in temporary opposition.

Jacob, the son of Isaac and Rebekah, the grandson of Abraham and Sara, is difficult from the very beginning. Even in the womb of his mother he struggles with his twin brother, Esau, to be born first. Esau wins that round, and because he is born first, he has the right to be his father's heir.

Later, however, Jacob shrewdly tricks Esau out of his birthright as well as their father's final blessing. It is a hollow victory for Jacob. Because of Esau's hostility, he is forced to flee the country, an exile from the land in which the promises of God were to be fulfilled. In his new wilderness, Jacob comes into great wealth, partially through devious means. He also acquires two wives. With his riches, he now determines to go home and win over Esau by lavish gifts.

On the way home, God appears to Jacob in a dream, taking the form of a man. The man wrestles with Jacob until daybreak. The wrestling is hardly described, but it is significant. Jacob finally receives a blessing from his opponent, but he walks away limping from the combat. Just prior to that, a remarkable dialogue takes place in Chapter 32, verses 26–29, which follows in a free translation.

> *He (the man) said, "Let me go for the day is breaking." But Jacob said, "I will not let you go, unless you bless me." And he (the man) said to him, "What is your name?" And he said, "Jacob." Then he (the man) said, "Your name shall no more be called Jacob, but Israel, for you have striven with God and with men and have prevailed." Then Jacob asked him "Tell me, I pray, your name." But he said, "Why is it that you ask my name?" And there he blessed him.*

Jacob holds his own throughout most of the struggle, but in the end the stranger wins on three counts. First, he wounds

Jacob in the hip, leaving him with a limp; second, he gives Jacob a new name; and third, he refuses to reveal who he is.

The limp is the scar Jacob carries from the struggle. It will be a reminder, a point of remembering the place where his life took a sharp turn. The new name implies he is a new being with a changed identity. He had been Jacob—heel, trickster, overreacher, supplanter—but now he becomes Israel—God rules, God preserves, God protects. In the act of wrestling, some of the power of God invaded the weakness of Jacob, and Jacob finally received the blessing that he had ardently craved all his life. But he is not allowed to penetrate the mystery. God remains the Inscrutable, the Infinite Other, who is gracious even while hidden.

Jacob then goes home with a new power, the power of a faith rekindled and a love reborn. He no longer has a need to repress his power against his brother. He is touchingly reconciled to Esau and begins his new life.

Geoffrey Wainwright, in his comprehensive and scholarly book on worship, includes wrestling as the last of the eight attitudes that typically occur in Christian worship and that express various facets of the relationship between God and humanity.[1] I say it is also one of the attitudes of the contemplative life, for we are all, at various times in life, thrust into opposition against God and left to wrestle with the mysterious and inscrutable behavior of a God we neither fully know nor are able to control. Wrestling may seem a strange component of spirituality, but I am convinced it is inevitable. If we are going to become voluntary and cooperative partners with God in completing the grand design of creation, we may first need to show our mettle and challenge God at the deepest level of our pain and anger.

Sometime or another each one of us will wrestle with God, often at the point where we must face our aloneness. That word rings a death knell for us. Who wants to be alone, other than the oddities who seek existence as recluses or hermits? Yet the word alone has a meaning from the old English that ought to settle over us like a mantle of comfort—*All plus one*. No matter how rich and satisfying life may be, there comes a time when we are coerced to see ourselves as separate and independent from everyone else. In that aloneness we begin to see the All and gradually accept the fact that we are each a piece of the Whole, an integer in the universe. As we become conscious of the One, which is the principle of treasuring, we learn to accept the All. This is the principle of connecting.

Connecting, however, does not eliminate the spiritual aspect of wrestling. That wrestling is usually precipitated by a relationship failure, perhaps in marriage, in our families, with our friends, or at the workplace. Or it may be brought on by the fact we have no meaningful relationships. Whatever cause, we come to a place in life where we know that what we have had so far has not been enough. We may be afflicted with remorse because of failures, missed opportunities, or what we term bad luck and persecution by others. We may think no one really understands us and that we are essentially an island in an uncaring sea of humanity.

This state can be with us for a long time. Indeed, we can even grow accustomed to it and draw upon our pain for survival. But one day something happens. We find ourselves alone, perhaps on the bank of a river as did Jacob, and we are so assailed with emptiness that we fear to go on. At that point, we may choose to die, thinking this will end the pain. Or we can begin wrestling with the law that commands us from within. If we choose to wrestle, we will begin to feel all our values turning themselves inside out, for our struggle is really with the law of our being.

Breakthrough usually comes in spite of ourselves. This happens at the place where "we know that we don't know," that we don't have all the answers and that we don't even know the right names for God. Breakthrough emerges from the unknown, just as revelation comes out of mystery. Slowly we begin to let go of our obsessions and fears, and as we do, we are given grace.

I remember a time when, as a child, I was afraid of the dark. Learning not to be afraid was not easy, but I finally overcame my fear by moving directly into the shadows, to assure myself there was no menacing figure lurking therein. Gradually I began to trust the dark, eventually to love it, and finally to be loved by it.

So we must wrestle with the dark side of our individual nature, until we finally come to the place where we trust ourselves, trust each other and trust the world. If we really believe we can trust the universe, we will cease to wrestle. But for most of us such a proposition cannot be simply accepted at face value or because someone tells us it is so. It has to be won through experience, through wrestling with doubts that have sought to persuade us that the universe is a hostile, alien place.

Once we make our contact with the ultimate Source of all things—even if it is in combat—our true self will emerge and a new quality of being will begin to manifest itself. We may limp and carry scars, but we will move forward with a confidence that cannot be defeated. We will have examined the place where we stand and will have finally grasped the Truth that the universe is gracious and that love is everywhere we are.

The unknown author of the classic *The Cloud of Unknowing* says that we must pass into the very thing that gives its name to the title of his book, forgetting everything we know about ourselves and our world, including our very existence. The author calls this act the cloud of forgetting. As we strain every nerve in every possible way to forget ourselves, we will encounter the ineffable God as an experience of love. Thus we will have a real knowledge of who God is and begin to experience ourselves as we really are.[2]

As I have said, there is a momentum in the spiritual life that is always asking us to let go and to let ourselves be carried along by Something greater than ourselves. But, oh, the struggle to yield, to let go! We want focus, clarity and inward vision rather than the impulse to move forward in a world that seems bent upon expansion and dimension. So we are often rendered immobile, unable to allow the momentum of spirit to carry us forward. Such a place is the arena for wrestling, for the soul can be satisfied with inertness and inactivity for only so long a time; then it will force us to make choices, even if all the choices look risky and uncertain.

It is wonderful for us to know that in essence we are never alone. No matter where we are or what we are doing, there is always present something more than ourselves at any given moment. As Howard Thurman reminds us, "Always we are visited."[3] That visit may be an idea that penetrates from beyond without any apparent connection to our past, or it may emerge from the cumulative energy of a memory. That visit may take the shape of a stranger on our path or an old friend coming forth in quiet response to our unspoken need. Always we are visited, and the visitor is God in some form or another. Occasionally the visit may precipitate a struggle. The door that is opened by the struggle may lead us into a temple of light, but the vestibule is dark and dismal. We do not want to cross through the dark hallway to reach the lighted room. We want to know the ultimate meaning of things, we want to move out from under the weight of our burdens and the ordeals of life, but we want to do so without too much struggle or sacrifice.

Such is the human dilemma. We cannot turn our moments of depression and despair into moments of joy and delight without struggling in the dark with a God we do not know and cannot understand. We fear the God of our childhood, who is "way off there," above the sky, who deals with us harshly when we violate "his" commandments. We are not even sure we want to be intimate with such a God. So we wrestle, imprisoned and body-bound, in an attempt to touch the starry robe of a new God, a God who is loving and understanding. It is in the great drama of that wrestling that our life gradually passes from its old grief into quiet, tender joy. We merge our tiny parts into the Great Whole, we open our little selves to the Infinite Much.

God cares enough for us to wrestle with us! Over the battle-field stretches this Divine Truth, softening, reconciling, forgiving. Our earthly life begins to touch the infinite unknown, and the new God comes.

We may not have an answer to our dilemma, but we have found a transcending. We may go on asking the questions that cannot be answered, and we may keep on creating the problems that cannot be solved. But we will slowly pass beyond the stage in which answers and solutions are burning necessities. The time will come when we will look back from a distance and say, "Well, I'm through with that phase." Thus we transcend our obsessive concerns with ourselves and begin to take on the nobler burden of caring for others and their tribulations. And all this because we "have striven with God and with men and have prevailed."

This was precisely the pilgrimage of Jacob. His personal tribulations and selfish hopes had traveled by his side to the point where he finally reached the end of his self's little circle.

He saw that the separation between his brother and himself had produced his greater separation from God. As he wrestled, he found himself in contact with the God in whom he lived and moved and had his being. And thus he found the wider spiritual life that set him free. In his trying to hold fast to God, because he was afraid God would run away before blessing him, Jacob learned that we cannot clutch at God with the hands of a greedy heart. God cannot be possessed by such. Moreover, God is neither distant nor unreal. God is the Infinite who cannot be touched and the Inscrutable who cannot be named, but the Friend who is right there in the midst of the choked-up, empty heart, ready to bestow the blessing. God is All. And when we are alone, God is in the midst of us, *All plus one*.

It is somewhat easy to write of this now, but it has not always been so. At no level in my life have I argued and wrestled more vigorously with God than at the level of my calling into the ministry. When I was in high school, and a well-meaning, earnest pastor suggested that I ought to consider my talents as peculiarly adapted for ministry, I knew that it was the last thing I wanted to do. Yet the suggestion would not go away. I found myself wrestling angrily with the question that was posed as a result of my decision to be a Christian. I will not do *it*, I vowed fervently; *it* is not for me.

My struggle was not because I did not love God or because I was innately recalcitrant. It was rather because I viewed the ministry as dull and oppressive, requiring a false persona. It seemed removed from the real world. I saw a pastor as one limited by the whims and vagaries of a congregation, most of whom japed and scorned him behind his back and directed intolerance and censoriousness to his face. I now realize I viewed the ministry through a skewed and inaccurate perspective, but I was sure I did not want it.

Following three years of teaching, two in Stanley and one in the seventh grade in Arco, I went back to Linfield for the completion of my college education. I fulfilled the requirements to be a high school teacher of English and music and returned to Arco, this time to teach in the high school. Yet nothing was settled. I knew deep down I was just marking time and that while I enjoyed teaching, it would not be my life profession. It was strange to think that way about something I liked rather well, but I did.

One day, partway through my third year of teaching at that high school, I stood at the classroom window watching large snowflakes fall from the sky and mount one upon the other atop an already frozen mantle of ice and drifted snow. I thought how fragile was a single snowflake but how mighty they became when amassed. I wondered, Is that the way of this universe? Do we only become strong when we unite? Are we nothing until then?

It was fourth-period junior English, a class made up predominantly of boys, most of them with behavior problems. Singly no boy in that class was a menace. Together they were formidable opponents to structure and rules. I had a better than average ability to get along with that sort of student, of holding them to a required modicum of social behavior, but I was intensely weary from the effort. And I had yet to find a way to motivate them when it came to learning how to appreciate and use their language with skill and accuracy.

With my back to them, I heard the shuffling and whispering start and begin to spread. I knew if it were not checked, the room would eventually erupt into pandemonium. But for a few moments I continued to stare out the window at the falling snow, my spirit more there than in the room. As I watched flake fall upon flake, I had a sudden burst of insight: *I will not be doing this anymore!* My pleasant but short-lived teaching career was coming to an end. I saw what it would be like if I stayed. In another ten years of trying to stuff grammar into unwilling minds or elicit music from untrained voices I would be an embittered, frustrated man. There is nothing wrong with teaching. It was just not my calling. I was still young. I wanted to see more of the world and experience new dimensions of life. I had to leave. So quick and complete was my decision that I had an impish impulse to swing around and announce it to the class, but I knew that would not be appropriate.

I turned just in time to catch Herb Strong in the process of shooting a note across the room to Lee Nelson. Caught in the act, Herb blushed and ducked his head into his binder, pretending to search for the composition paper I knew he did not have—in fact, never had. In the joy of my newfound freedom and in the realization that soon I would no longer have to play the "heavy" to juvenile truants, I walked down the aisle and laid my hand affectionately on Herb's neck and its carefully swept ducktails of glistening hair. I felt the boy tense under the unaccustomed touch. "Thank you, Herb," I said quietly. He did not know it, but he had helped seal my decision. I passed on, leaving him confused and immobile for the rest of the hour.

Many of my decisions are hammered out through long hours of weighing and balancing. Not that one. It came clear to me in a single moment that I was going to do something else. What that would be was not yet certain. What were my options? Graduate school. A year in Europe. Seminary. Ugh! Not seminary. But though I wrote to several universities for information about graduate programs, the notion of seminary kept hammering at me incessantly. Be fair, I cautioned myself. Look in all directions. So I wrote to a Baptist seminary in Boston about the possibility of a scholarship. I didn't really need the latter just then, but my rigid resistance to the prospect demanded that I create some hurdles. Within a few months I was accepted at the seminary with the promise of some financial aid. A year in Boston sounded adventuresome.

Summer came. I said good-bye to my students for the last time. "How will I make it through senior English without you?" moaned Herb in mock distress, unwilling to show that any teacher had elicited his appreciation. "You may not," I bantered, remembering that he had come within a hair of flunking under me. Then I joyously realized I was no longer responsible for anyone making it through English.

With time on my hands that summer, I accepted the opportunity to counsel at a church youth camp a few miles above Sun Valley. It was there I met a minister named Walt Pulliam, a few years older than I. He was then pastoring in Caldwell and was destined someday to become the president of the American Baptist Churches USA. Walt was a graduate of the Baptist seminary in Berkeley. "Why go so far away?" he queried, when I told him I planned to attend the seminary in Boston next year. "It will be difficult to get placed in a church on the West Coast from an eastern school."

"I'm not sure I want placement," I said. "My future plans are unsettled right now. I just thought I'd try a year of seminary and see how I got on."

"Wouldn't hurt to explore Berkeley," he suggested. "It's not only a fine school, it has the warm feel of a family among its students and faculty."

In the week I worked with Walt at that camp I came to like him immensely. His statement of "the warm feel of a family" stayed with me. Who doesn't want that? It's what we are made for. I wrote to the dean at the American Baptist Seminary in Berkeley in late July, less than six weeks before school was to open, and was accepted. Instead of Boston, I went to Berkeley. Considering my starting point was Arco, I was making progress.

Sometimes life decisions are built on such casual whims that we wonder if there is a right or wrong way to go in life. Yet I am convinced that every decision we make, no matter how insignificant or capricious, is part of our soul's work. Wrong decisions may alter the plan, but they cannot destroy it, for the plan is part of that infinite presence of the not-yet-known that engages us to reach into the depths and find what we are and what we are supposed to do. I needed to serve something higher than myself. Yet I needed to explore the horizons of my knowing, even while establishing my stifled and unexplored self into the framework of its plan. Something mysterious and wonderful seemed to be guiding me.

My three years at a seminary were not only intellectually and spiritually stimulating, I felt I belonged to a group of people who shared a common call and vision. My call was still not clear, but I was now willing to consider some form of ministry. I thought of the mission field but knew it was the idea of travel that appealed, not the work. I had several invitations to consider positions in the areas of youth ministry or Christian education, but I felt no real impulse to pursue those. A small church on the plains of North Dakota was willing to risk considering me as their pastor, but the plains of North Dakota were not exactly what I had in mind. In short, I was unbearably hard to please because I had still not fully accepted or defined my call.

Then a few weeks before graduation, I read in the newspaper of interviews being conducted at the University of California for teachers and counselors in American schools in Europe. These schools were maintained for dependents of U.S. military personnel stationed overseas. I marched straight down to the campus for an interview, and before it was over, I knew I had been accepted. Formal verification followed a few weeks later. I was happy and relieved. The issue of ministry was not settled. The wrestling would continue. But for now I was happy. My hunger for travel was about to be met.

My assignment was Verdun, France. I was counselor for high school boys who came from several Army and Air Force bases in eastern France to attend high school. It was not unlike work I was used to, with a few more Herbs to try to mold and shape. But I reveled in the opportunity to experience another culture and to practice my college French to my heart's content.

Verdun, located on the Meuse River, is a picturesque but peculiar town. It figuratively exists now as a monument to war. Because of its strategic location near the German border, it was the scene of some of the bloodiest and lengthiest battles of both World Wars. Cemeteries of the war dead stretch for miles on the outskirts of the town, and at one of these burial grounds stands a huge stone structure that houses the bones of thousands of soldiers who were buried in a common grave because they could not be individually identified. Here I spent a year, from which I was able to travel to most of the countries of western Europe. It was a gracious moratorium to my wrestling over the confused issue of ministry.

That winter in Verdun was harsh and cold. The countryside became gray and barren, but when spring came, the hills and fields burst into life. I never cease to marvel at the miracle of spring. How a world can lie under the frozen blanket of winter for months and then suddenly spring back to life continues to thrill and amaze me. It is all perfectly explainable, but it impresses me as a parable of the latent unformed divinity in the human creature. That divinity needs to grow, and it will, despite long seasons of dormancy and numbness. Then comes the seeking, the questioning, the hunger for being and truth, and divinity is manifested in everyday life in no less startling ways than spring returning to a frigid earth.

One brilliant day I hiked up in the rolling hills west of Verdun. The country there is pockmarked with old shell craters and foxholes, and because of mines that have not been detonated, the land lies useless and virtually uninhabited. I kept carefully to the road until suddenly I came to its end. It opened out into a clearing in the trees, where stood a wee stone chapel. As I read the inscription on the chapel, I learned that here in this clearing had once existed a small village. It had been totally destroyed in World War II. Every building had been leveled and the entire population either killed or driven away. The chapel had been built to commemorate the fact that at one time on this spot a community of men, women and children had lived, loved and worked together.

I sat down on the stone steps of the tiny chapel and looked about me. A cool breeze stirred the grass at my feet. I saw that someone had planted a bed of irises beside the wall, some of which were struggling valiantly to bloom. But I had no appreciation for their efforts. The world had suddenly turned to ashes. I felt myself looking at a universe of shadows and cruelties, where life is essentially vain and empty. I sat there asking myself the question "What for?" Life seemed to have no meaning in that empty clearing where once people had pursued a living together only to have existence and hope snatched cruelly from them.

Then a presence seemed to step into that clearing. I had the sense I was not alone, that someone had joined me, was there even at that moment. Nothing physical was apparent, but I heard in my mind a question countering the one I had just asked, "*What are you going to do about it?*"

The sun started to sink by the time I got up to leave. I had no answer for either the question I had asked or the one asked of me. But I knew the wrestling had commenced in earnest. This time the issue was not just my calling but the more important consideration, does the world have meaning? And if it does, why do people kill each other, why is there pain and disease, what is the brain for? All these questions, emerging in the margins of that hour in the woods, were impelling me to face my own wish for Being, the striving to meet the God known in the ancient traditions of faith, and the perplexing and annoying call that I was somehow destined to serve God with my vocation. *"What are you going to do about it?"* Evading and temporizing were over. The question demanded an answer.

The school year ended. I left Verdun and drove to Le Harve to meet Gary, a friend from the States who had come to Europe to spend the summer traveling with me. We explored the Scandinavian countries before swinging south to Switzerland. I wanted to see the Matterhorn.

Gary was a good traveling companion. He was cheerful, willing to let me choose directions and select agenda. He was also sensitive to the fact that I was limping emotionally. Some of the reasons I could share with him; some I could not. I was at that time in receipt of a letter from a church in Oakland, inquiring if I would be interested in a position on the staff as an assistant minister, with some responsibilities in music. Returning to the Bay Area held an unmistakable appeal, but how could I be sure about the church? It was like jumping into a pool of water that is over your head when you aren't sure how well you can swim.

I was also trying desperately to have faith in something I could not know or control. I wanted God to become an intimate acquaintance, not a distant stranger or an outmoded concept that my mind had long left behind. I wanted to find a way of being where I could become a point of intercession between this world and the next for broken, despairing people. I wanted a sense of objectivity toward myself and a vision of what I had come on this earth to do. I wanted much, and I was exhausted with wrestling. I was scarred, unworthy, nearly defeated, but, like Jacob, I still demanded a blessing.

When we arrived at Zermatt, the alpine village snuggled at the base of the Matterhorn, we felt an overwhelming sense of disappointment that the peak had been swaddled in fog for several days. We had planned only a day there. While we were willing to extend this if necessary, we were not encouraged to learn from one American couple, who had been there three days, that they had yet to see the mountain that lures visitors from all over the world. It had stubbornly remained enshrouded.

We walked disconsolately around the winding streets of the picturesque village, peering in its shops and sampling the incomparable Swiss chocolate. At length I suggested to Gary we separate for a couple of hours, to come back together at a later time. We would then make our decision about whether to seek overnight accommodations or return down the cogwheel railway to our car and proceed into Italy.

I was strongly feeling the need to be alone. So many concerns were whirling through my mind at that time—Verdun and its incompleted aspects of relationships; the letter from the Oakland church awaiting my answer and arousing the peroration against my calling to ministry; and the awareness that after being in Europe for a year, I was viscerally homesick. All of these pressed on my spirit in competition with the conviviality of the adventure.

Alone, on a grassy slope at the edge of the village, I sat down. I looked across a valley to the fog bank that was creating a momentary reversal of our plans and shutting me out from seeing the mountain that I had long held in imaginative vision.

We all know the phenomenon of waking from sleep to find the answer to a problem we could not solve the day before. This happens because everything we need lies within us. Self-knowledge is the key ingredient, for decision making always uses the raw material that arises from the details of our self-awareness. As I sat there, I was longing for that unknown person within me to emerge and help me make the right choices. Yet at the same time I was a little fearful to embrace that quality within myself that had the power to carry me beyond the little walls in which I was enclosed at that moment.

Prayer, at that point in my life, was more an activity reserved for my undiscovered self than something with which I was intimately familiar. That is, I had always felt when I prayed that I was involved in an unreal activity that was conducted by some stranger within me. I had yet to awaken to the fact that something greater than my design or effort is at work when I pray and that prayer is simply a stepping aside to allow God to work. But prayer, whether rightly understood or not, is native to all of us. In our moments of greatest extremities we are all inclined to make banquets from whatever crumbs we can find. Put us in a foxhole of any kind and we will usually pray. Hence, it was of no particular surprise to find myself wanting to pray at that moment. Like anyone else, I wanted to position myself as favorably as possible in the direction where the cooling breezes are most likely to blow.

I lowered my head and closed my eyes, earlier disciplines having taught me that is the acceptable posture. But I could not form any words beyond my first reflex, "O God." I had so long ignored the connection between grace and discipline that now when I came to reach for one I was so unskilled at the other that I knew not how to do more than mutely stretch forth the arms of my soul. I waited, feeling awkward and uncertain, remembering an earlier time when a pastor had prayed for me to find my way.

Then with the return of that memory came another. In a long ago sermon by that same pastor I had met Gideon, the Hebrew farmer turned soldier, who delivered his nation from annual raids by the Midianites (Judges 6:11–8:35). Those camel raiders had made existence precarious for the Israelite farmers who had settled adjacent to the desert. Since it was really a conflict between Yahwehism and Baalism, Gideon turned to Yahweh, the God of his people, for strength to contend against the pagan forces of Baal. He said to God, "If you really wish to deliver my people, then prove yourself by this test. I will lay a fleece of wool on the threshing floor; if there is dew on the fleece in the morning and the ground is dry, then I will know you are with us." I remember the preacher in Arco saying at that point, "So Gideon did, and in turn, God did." Gideon, not yet satisfied or convinced, wanted to make sure he wasn't being deceived. He asked that the following morning the fleece be dry and the ground wet. And again, "God did." So Gideon led his army to battle, and they defeated the Midianites forever.

One has to suspend temporarily many modern concepts about God and see this story from the standpoint of an ancient people's faith. Gideon found the sign he needed to help him go on. The slaughter of the Midianite soldiers may offend our sensibilities as a work of God, but there is no denial that Gideon's army felt God-empowered and brought an end to the raids. "Sometimes," said the Reverend Gerald Dryden, "there are occasions in life when we have a right to lay the fleece."

Was this such a time, I wondered? Here on the foothills of the Matterhorn could I dare ask for a sign? Before my conscious mind could move in with its arguments, I raised my eyes and, looking across the valley of mist, I heard myself saying, "O God, if you want me to go to that church in Oakland, let me see that mountain."

How can I describe what happened next and make you see it as I saw it then, as I am seeing it now? Quietly, simply, the clouds began to drift apart. Within a few seconds the Matterhorn stood before me in its naked, rugged splendor.

It is difficult to explain all that happened to me in that moment. I was like a person who had been trying to cross a flooded stream and looking for a secure place to put my feet, when suddenly I found myself standing on solid ground on the other side. I seemed to have pushed beneath the accumulated layers of ego-identity to find myself at the deep level of being. There were no more places to go. I was no longer seeking answers with which I would not be able to live if they were suddenly given. I had simply come to that place where I was willing to take whatever came with great trust. The world was no longer a fearful, empty place. A quiet awe mingled with a great gratitude began to sing within me. That such an oblique prayer as the one I had casually hurled in the direction of that mountain should pour out such peace upon me was nothing I could justify or explain. I could only accept. In my silence I faced the mystery, not even comprehending the depths of the moment and certainly not the depths of God's infinite purpose. Yet for a moment I was transcended above my need to know.

I remember Annie Dillard in one of her books talked about silence bashing her broadside from the heavens and God saying, "I am here, but not as you have known me." She turned away, willful, and the whole thing vanished as the realness of things disassembled. So I knew I would not be able to hold forever that moment when acres of open sky, clear and still, invited me to see the shape of a mountain peak. Its poise and stillness were unendurable, anyway. Yet long after the mountain had faded from view, I would know that the eternity and peace of God had somehow invaded my life secretly, and that I had been found eternally as I was meant to be.

I returned to the United States and took the assignment at the Lakeshore Avenue Baptist Church in Oakland. There began eighteen happy and productive years of life and ministry. Within a year of my starting as the assistant minister, I became the senior minister. The details are no less wonderful than that which preceded it, but they do not belong here.

Like Jacob, I came home reconciled and at peace with myself. I did not come home with a wife, as did Jacob (in fact, he had two of them). But I did meet Beverly shortly after, and a year later we were married. She was and is the greatest gift of all.

Would I never have to wrestle again with God? There is no end to the wrestling, at least as far as I can see. Certain things are ineluctable, not to be resisted. Perhaps God is one of these things, but not yet have I completely ceased wrestling or resisting. The shimmering waters in front of my house, dancing with the widening lake of sky above my head, which always sets loose in me the need to dance and at the same to kneel, is just one more sign of the great looming presence of God that never ceases for a moment to draw surrender from me. I have not fully let go of that dictator self that always tries to take over the controls and prevent me from listening. But I have crept enough times to the altar to offer myself that my resistance is being gradually and gently worn down.

We have an inner history as well as an outer one. Giving attention to the Matterhorn that day transformed me to a place of giving myself more fully to the world. When I finally achieved the courage to share the experience in a sermon, a brash young seminary student challenged me at the door as he was leaving the church and unknowingly helped me place the experience in its outer framework.

"Do you really think your prayer made the clouds move?" he asked skeptically, his tone indicating disdain for the possibility.

I had never really thought about it before. It hadn't mattered. Every step proceeding from that moment had been so eminently right that I had had no reason to deny or doubt what had happened. Now I was being forced to offer a rationale to something that defied reason.

I heard myself answering, "No, I don't really think that was what happened. The clouds would probably have moved anyway. The miracle is not that my prayer moved the clouds. The miracle was rather that I was moved, moved to pray in such a manner that my prayers were coincidental to the appearance of that mountain."

He looked puzzled and passed on, not sure what I meant. But now I knew what had eluded me earlier. Prayer is not what I do. It is what God does. And all my feeble efforts to pray are simply responses to a God who never ceases to yearn over me and draw me to Godself. Prayer is not remaking the universe to fit my plans. Prayer is fitting into the universe and seeing in each movement and circumstance, even in the parting of clouds, the sign of the eternal presence that illuminates my darkness and enlarges my way of being.

I know now there exists something in this world that one might call clarity. Its message can be carried in a single blade of grass, a human being or the vastness of a countryside. It matters not where we find it, for it is everywhere. What matters is that we finally come to understand there is a reality that exists eternally in God, undivided by space, time or any other limitation. There is a Matterhorn, but the way in which it might appear to me may be illusory. What matters is not the mountain itself but the integral vision that grasps the universe as a whole, rather than the detail of its parts, and begins to experience indivisible unity. When we grasp life in this manner, there comes a clarity that helps us begin to know ourselves. And in knowing ourselves, we begin to experience God and each other in more deeply meaningful ways.

We each have our own demons with which we must wrestle. For some it is the demon of impatience, a fierce and willful force inside that refuses to let us rest. Mine has not only been the demon of impatience, it has also been the demon of inadequacy. "Hurry up!" yells one demon, while the other cries, "Not good enough!"

May Sarton, American writer and poet, notes that there are no quick rewards for a demon-possessed person. It is a matter of making a channel and then guiding one's boat day by day. Her channel was her work, her writing. But even though she was happy while writing, once it was down on paper, the critic would take over from the creator, and she had a new demon to wrestle.[4]

I resonate with her words. I have spent a lifetime wrestling with my demons of impatience, insecurity, inferiority and occasionally anger. I have prepared and delivered sermons now for forty years. My preparation is always painstaking and conscientious, and I try to make my delivery the same. Yet a critical word from a listener has had the power to destroy the effort in a moment. Through the years my critics have intensified rather than lessened, since my theology did not always follow old traditions. But gradually and inexorably I have been able to realize a modicum of peaceful defense within myself that remains essentially unscathed. It has been a long, hard battle, and I cannot yet claim full victory. But I am now more at peace with myself and hence content to leave my efforts behind without bemoaning or regretting that which cannot be changed. I am finally able to refuse control by the critics and retain for myself the right to believe in myself rather than letting anyone diffuse that by words of disagreement or dissatisfaction.

The tensions that precipitate our wrestling are normal and healthy. We are only in danger if we turn away from the challenges and refuse to battle our way toward a true self-understanding and into life-at-large. Our refusal to wrestle makes us prey to destructive forces. We may claim to believe in God, but, to paraphrase Basque Catholic writer Unamuno, if we have no passion in our hearts, no anguish and uncertainty in our minds, no doubt and even despair in our actions, then we believe only in some concrete idea of God rather than in a God of mystery and love.

Do we want a cardboard God? Or do we want a God who will come and wrestle with us through our conflict and doubt, who will perhaps wound us in the struggle but bless us in the end? That is the whole meaning of Gethsemane and Cavalry. Real faith, as Jesus showed in the garden and on the cross, is recognizing doubt as an essential and important component of the spiritual life and wrestling through to the place where we can declare, "Into thy hands I commend my spirit." At that point the demons with which we have long wrestled will become the angels that come to bless us, and the wilderness that once terrified us will become our true home.

A Prayer of Wrestling

You have the advantages and the edge on us, God. Whoever or whatever you are, there is no way we can match our puny strength with yours. I believe I can tell you anything and everything and that you will still love me. Yet I am scared of the subtleties of life. I am scared of what's expected of me. I am scared of the pushing, the pulling, the pressures. I wonder if I have any real control over my life. I want to find out a little more of what it means to live under your blessing. Help me look honestly at myself, as honestly as you look, and to love myself as deeply as you love me. Grant me new freedom this day from my constant struggling. And let your peace be mine, as indeed it already is. Through Christ. Amen.

Spiritual Exercises
for
Wrestling

1. Ask yourself three questions, answering quickly with your first impulse rather than after a lot of rational consideration. Jot your answers in your journal, realizing they are revealing glimpses of the issues with which you wrestle.

   a. Would I rather march in a peace rally or spend an hour praying for peace?

   b. If I were hiking and came to a fork where one trail led up a mountainside and the other fork led down into a valley, which would I take?

   c. Who would be the last person I would choose as a walking or traveling companion and why?

2. Over the next several days or weeks, as you go about, be alert to the rocks or stones you see on the ground. Many may catch your eye, but one will "call" you. In effect, some stone will choose you, rather than you choosing this stone. Take this stone home, perhaps washing or wiping it clean. Then find some time to be alone with the stone. Hold it in your hands, allowing the stone to speak to you. As your hands warm the stone, through your tactile connection to this inanimate object seek connection to the God who created both you and the stone. Let the stone become an

altar where all your struggles can be offered up to God. You may wish to think of it as a healing stone, placing it upon those places on your body where you are experiencing pain or discomfort. Record your insights in your spiritual journal. You may wish to keep the stone, or at some point you may wish to return it to nature with reverence and thanks for what it has given you.

14

Waiting

Blessed are those who wait upon God,
for they shall renew their strength and deepen their faith.

I am back at my post watching the Puget Sound from my window. I study it intently, thinking that perhaps the simple, absolute and immutable mysteries of Truth are hidden somewhere in those super luminous waves that roil with beauty, as though a thousand silver salmon are swimming beneath their surface. Those waves, careening toward me across a watery meadow with all its shapes and growing, seem to take on the quality of an infinite font of flickering, broken wings that fill my unseeing mind with splendors of translucent beauty.

I have a season ticket at this salt-air theater. The performance here is always fresh and full of incredible promise, for concealed under all this natural light must be the way that leads from petty particulars to universal wonders. Everything that touches me here seems rooted in the touch of the Absolute God, and I can agree with whoever it was that said, "It is a vast creation, but a vaster salvation."

This sea in front of me seems to offer the astonishing gift of salvation lived in joyous uncertainty. In this one moving current I bring all events (cosmic and cellular), all persons (living and dead), all life (sentient and nonsentient), all ideas (cognitive and ruminative), all prayers (silent and spoken), until everything rises and falls together on the strength of these waves. Here everything touches me, and I touch everything. Here everything is interjoined and interpenetrated in the ebb and flow of the tides into one unitary experience. So here I wait, as a scientist waits at the laboratory, for meaning to evolve from research into real life. Here I wait, as a communicant waits at the altar for a revelation of Truth from God.

But this sea in front of me also limits me. While I wait for Truth to enter my mind from this illuminated manuscript of a pool, softly and persistently something else invades. It is silence. Interestingly enough, it is not the silence of absence but the silence of presence. Something is coming to me across that slate-blue patch of salt water, something that may not unfold theorems of truth but will season my day. But who? What? I wait, and nothing comes. No truth is revealed. No one arrives. Only silence. Yet out of the silence, Something.

I am not always a patient person. Impatience is one of my demons, as I told you earlier. I sometimes find it difficult to follow the dictates of the poet John Burroughs who said, "Serene, I fold my hands and wait, knowing that my own will come to me." (paraphrased). Even as I wait, I am tense, poised to leap, rippling with inner currents of activity.

Who decided that silence is quietness, nothingness, serenity? The flood that passes through me in these moments of waiting is no less spectacular than the ocean that writhes at my feet. I am a crossroads for fugitives of the sacred and the secular, transients from the holy and the profane, visitors from the natural and the supernatural. They move over and through me as though I were a city where all the main roads of commerce converge. And although the mystery of this traffic is delicately veiled from me, I feel it pass like phantom whispers against the tracery of my mind, until gradually I am pointed not toward some otherness but toward the mysterious wonder that is around me and within me.

"They that wait for the Lord shall renew their strength, they shall mount up with wings like eagles, they shall run and not be weary, they shall walk and not faint" (Isaiah 40:31). These ancient words from the prophet were learned at the knee of some long-forgotten Sunday school teacher, who inspired me to rack up salvation credits with memory verses in the same way a schoolboy studies to pass an exam. They flit through my brain and send me scurrying back to the Bible commentaries to decipher the word *wait* from the Hebrew mind. I learn there are eight different words translated *wait* in the Old Testament, each of which is used in connection with prayer. One English word that means eight different things in Hebrew, the language in which the concept originated! Who can keep up with it? But then I discover that the most common meaning, and the one related to Isaiah's verse, is "to twist, stretch or put under tension." In at least one place (Psalm 37:7) it refers to the pain of childbirth.

Now a dynamic new concept of waiting emerges. It is not always standing still or stopping in one spot. It is occasionally being stretched on the gallows, tightened like a guitar string, twisted upon the spear of rejection, writhing under the accusations and persecutions of those who seek to destroy you. That explains why on certain days, when I place myself in front of my seaside altar, my mind is like a battlefield. On other days it is like a classroom. And on some days it is like a womb, where in the safety of darkness and stillness I am impregnated with a new wonder.

When we wait for God, we have no guarantee what will happen. Waiting could mean giving birth to a new idea. Waiting could mean watching, as if from hiding, as we make intercession for the broken and bruised ones of the world. Waiting could mean sticking tenaciously to the job at hand. Or it could mean to twist, stretch or writhe under the tension of life pulling in many directions at once.

To practice waiting, in order to achieve a life free from tension and conflict, is to achieve something other than a real human life. Real life is always lived somewhere between knowing and not knowing, having and not having. We advance more from the point of our conflicts than from the point of our victories. We live more from our questions than from our answers. The energy for growth comes from the pull of the opposing parts of our experience, and waiting is where we find the exhilaration for keeping on, rather than dropping out.

Eighteen years of my life, from 1962 to 1980, were lived as the pastor of the Lakeshore Avenue Baptist Church in Oakland, California. I can look back now on those years as idyllic, almost dreamlike in their contentment. We tend to forget the pain and conflict that is the inevitable part of all living. I know these were present, but I was so surprised by the joy I found in being a pastor, after wrestling for years against the notion, that the blessings of those Oakland years far outweigh the adversities. I grew with the church. In fact, we grew with each other. We built on the foundations of faith that others before us had created, and together we established a vibrant community of faith and caring that was solidly interracial.

But there came a day when the traffic signal began to turn green. Something said it was time to move. I was back again to wrestling. It was wrestling that had brought me to Oakland. Would wrestling take me from there? Nothing was really wrong. I was happy. The church was happy. We had no immense problems. Financially everything was solvent and secure, and spiritually we had grown into a loving, inclusive fellowship of persons of all races and lifestyles. If anything was wrong, maybe we had grown too complacent. Maybe the congregation had come to rely too much on me. And maybe I had become too comfortable, too secure in my power. Where there is no stress, we generally tend not to be as fully creative as we otherwise might.

Still, I probably would have done nothing (one does not destroy one's bed just because it makes him sleep soundly) had not an invitation come from the First Baptist Church in Seattle, Washington to consider being one of the candidates for pastor of that church. I was willing to let my name enter the ring, feeling fairly confident I would not be selected. Even though I was feeling a certain restlessness, I sincerely did not want to leave where I was. Could I not move inwardly to some new state of being and enthusiasm without changing my outer environment? I hoped so.

It was a long process. There were indeed many candidates to consider, and it took the better part of a year before the field was narrowed to four. To my amazement, I was one of the four. At an invitation from the search committee, I flew to Seattle for an interview, still not realizing that my life was about to undergo a drastic upheaval.

A few months later, there were only two of us being considered, and I was invited to come to Seattle and preach at a nearby church, where the committee could hear me and then spend an afternoon in dialogue with me. The day went pretty much as ordered. I preached a standard Romneyian fare of spirituality (which not everyone finds palatable), and we spent the afternoon in discussion. The members of the committee were stimulating and interesting people who obviously cared deeply for their church and wanted the best leadership for it.

At sunset I was on the plane flying back to Oakland, leaving them to make their choice. The weather was gray and overcast, but as the plane rose into the air, I saw the crest of Mount Rainier rising through the clouds in triumphant solitude. Its snow-daubed sides were covered with a marvelous rose patina created by reflection from the setting sun. One ought to do something with such beauty, I reasoned. But what to do but gaze in awe and stupefaction? I was glad to have no seatmate to distract me with conversation. I wanted to savor this moment alone. Most of all I wanted to gain perspective on what I should do if I were the candidate selected.

After gazing at this sky-splendor until it faded in the distance, I placed my head against the back of the seat and closed my eyes. It was like being back at the Matterhorn, except this time I didn't have to ask to see a mountain. It was already visible. And though I still needed guidance, I was spiritually richer and wiser than I had been at the Matterhorn. My prayer, however, was elementary. "Dear God, what do you want me to do?" We never grow too wise for that question.

I opened my eyes suddenly, with the strong impression someone had sat down in the seat beside me. But the seat was empty. Still the sense of Presence was unmistakable. I felt prickles rising on the back of my neck and between my shoulders. A flood of energy rippled through me like an electric current. Then I heard the words, not auditorially but in my mind, "*You don't have to go, but I want you to.*"

Someone has said that a revelation ought to be so clear that you cannot deny it. The sun is such a revelation. The mountain peaks of the Cascades are such a revelation. Pain is one. So is beauty. All authentic spirituality originates from revelation, the revealing of the mystical and the mysterious that lies beyond the reach of thinking and reasoning of any kind. Revelation is often the realm about which we can only speak with stammering uncertainty, because words have limited value when we try to force them to contain the mysteries. At best, our theologizing is suggestive rather than exhaustive, more often leading to a trivialization of the spiritual life rather than to a place of profound reverence. Still I must tell you that moment on the plane was for me a revelation, when God graciously offered me the options of moving or not but revealed which option represented the highest and best. I would have more than one occasion in the months ahead to go back and remember that moment.

After I arrived home that evening, I sat in the living room with Beverly and shared what the day had been like. I even dared to say that I thought they were going to ask me to be the next pastor of the Seattle church. As we were discussing what such a move would mean for us (she had a position as Home Economics department head in a junior high school), the telephone rang. It was the chairman of the search committee in Seattle, telling me that the committee had voted to call me as their next pastor.

The pain of leaving was incredible. I never knew it would be so hard. But how could it be otherwise? When something is loved, letting it go is extremely difficult, even though letting go is part of life's design. It seems to me that a 'Yes' is required of us at every stage of life, a 'Yes' to both life and death. There is an element of death in the letting-go experience, and all of life is training us how to die. In preparing for the masterpiece of a grand and supreme death, we go through many smaller deaths. Some of these deaths are petty, some are great. Leaving Lakeshore was a great death, and I had to wrestle with the thought that conscious dying is an all right thing to do.

I don't know why we humans struggle so at this level. Death is the most ancient and fundamental of all our biologic functions. When you place it on a spiritual level, it is so much at the heart of what Jesus taught that you are quite simply and naturally led to the realization that out of death comes life, just as out of emptiness comes fullness. Beneath the quiet waiting of a person always lies the potential of vigorous, creative action. In the experience of dying, no matter the level, always comes the experience of birthing. We've simply got to work on these precepts until we get them down inside our thinking where they belong. Then we can approach our various levels of death with greater acceptance and anticipation.

After I announced my resignation at Lakeshore and went through the first onslaught of grieving with the congregation, I settled down to the practical tasks of selling our home and sorting through, saving and discarding the accumulation of eighteen years. One day I was in the church office, cleaning out my desk, when I heard the office door open. Through the open door I could hear the voice of an elderly woman asking to see Dr. Romney. The secretary explained I had resigned and was moving. "I know that," said the woman snappishly. "I have listened to him on the radio for eighteen years, so I know all about this move. I wanted to see him before he left."

I came down the stairs as she finished speaking. A radio listener for eighteen years deserved at least a moment of my time. She stood there on matchstick-thin legs, a wizened and ancient woman in a shapeless old coat. Her hands were twisted and gnarled from arthritis. In those crippled hands was a tiny brown book. She held it out to me without ceremony or false adulation over the fact that she was for the first time in the physical presence of a voice she had listened to for nearly two decades.

"I want you to have this book," she said bluntly. "It has been a standby for me for years. I have been told to pass it on to you, because there will come a time when you will need it." That was all. She asked nothing but that I take the book.

I thanked her and accepted the gift. I watched her leave slowly and carefully, realizing how much the effort to come had cost her in terms of physical strength. A taxi was waiting outside, and she was gone before I remembered to ask her name. The little brown book was titled *The Power Within*, compiled by Clara Endicott Sears and privately published in 1911. A brief thought on spirituality was offered for each day by various writers. I took the book with me to Seattle, but in the whirlwind of activities that followed I all but forgot about it.

I had a bittersweet start with Seattle First Baptist Church. Although there were many people who welcomed us with genuine affection and love, there was a small handful who did not. In my first six months as pastor of that church, most of that latter group left, because they found my more liberal theology and open, inclusive style unpalatable. I have since learned this is not uncommon with the arrival of a new pastor; persons unhappy or dissident for various reasons often find that a convenient time to clear out. As I watched the numbers dwindle and tried to fight off my sense of homesickness and grief over leaving a place where I had been loved and accepted, I turned within myself for God's support more fervently than I had done in many years. I recalled my revelation on the plane and was steadied by it. I knew I would make it and would be better for the experience. But I was not enjoying the process of getting to that place.

One morning, deeply discouraged after a visit with a family who was leaving and anxious over a forthcoming appointment with another who was contemplating the same, I sat at my desk wondering how long this would continue. My eye fell on the little brown book that had been given to me by an unnamed lady with crippled hands. I picked it up and opened it to the reading for that particular day. This is what it said:

> *When someone is angry with you, and fault is found with you, instead of beginning to defend yourself and to answer back in the same spirit, turn your attention inward, and down every resentful word with these words of St. Paul: "None of these things shall move me." Always speak the words silently, not aloud, else you antagonize the other. Practice repeating these words at the approach of every annoying thought, even the most trivial events of your life, for it is by control over one's self in the little things of life that one has self-possession when the great things are facing him.*[1]

Those simple words were like food for my starving soul. I realized that I had a center in me that was inviolate and protected against all outer attacks or inner doubts. Within me there was a place that could not be moved. God had prepared the way long ago for me to have this particular truth at the moment I needed it. I told myself, "Rodney, you are part of the creation, an embodiment of the Creator. So create. Create from that center that is untouched by all human enemies. Take up your fate, your lot, whatever you wish to call it, and create. And let nothing move you from the work God called you to do."

That day marked the turning point. A new confidence and vision was instilled in me. During the next six months the dissatisfied members who had left were replaced by vibrant, enthusiastic people who first came to visit and then stayed to join.

As long as the nature of our work is not better than the environment in which we live, we will continue in that environment. But the moment we begin to improve the vitality, the power and the efficiency of our personal action, we will create a better environment. We can pass through any experience if we realize that the power residing within us is equal to the occasion. Sometimes waiting is the only avenue by which that discovery is made, but when it is made, life becomes easier and happier for us. We realize that there is within us a resource for every need and that we need not be moved away from tapping into that resource. Then we can face the mean and the difficult with confidence that we will make it, for "none of these things" has the power to move us off center.

A common form of atheism is distrust of self. We all suffer from a lack of self-confidence in the inner voice of our own intelligence, which is God within. If God is without, God is equally within, else God does not fill all being. To doubt God outside of oneself has been classified as classic atheism. But it is also atheism to distrust God's reflection within. That is why I strongly believe that when we find our real self, which we also call the Christ self, we find God.

This was the theme of my second book, *Journey to Inner Space*, and it gave some fundamentalists quite a stir. A woman wrote a full chapter against me in one of her books, claiming that finding God within is the oldest lie of all. If that be so, then the Bible must also lie, for the references to the Christ within are numerous, especially in the epistles of Paul. By finding this divine self, or the Christ within, we find and fulfill the highest law of our being. Only when we are in harmony with this law are we really useful. If we turn to God and sincerely seek to reflect God from within, then what we do will be inspired rather than a bustling endeavor of sowing seed on shallow soil.

The first step toward freedom is waiting. Not the kind of waiting that tells African Americans to be patient and do nothing because freedom is coming. Racial freedom and equality will never come if we do nothing, for the threads of racism are too deeply woven in the fabric of social consciousness. Nor am I talking about the kind of waiting demonstrated by the disciples when they fell asleep in the garden while Jesus prayed. Jesus wanted them to watch with him for just one hour. He needed their supportive companionship as he waited for the peace and presence of God to fill him and guide him through his forth-coming trial and crucifixion. But the disciples could not wait, so they fell asleep. They missed a wonderful opportunity to share in the enlightenment Jesus received, as he finally prayed, "Not my will but thine be done."

If we wait truly, we shall live truly. This kind of waiting may be equated with listening. We quiet ourselves within and without, while at the same time stretching every nerve in the direction of the infinite. We are listening for even the smallest whisper that may come from the still small voice, even though we may be stretched on the gallows of persecution or twisted upon the spear of rejection.

The next step toward freedom is answering. Having waited until guidance comes, we are now ready to move out obediently and trustingly, even if it be to crucifixion. The truly teachable person is the one who not only waits to receive the truth but is also willing to act on it when it arrives.

A Prayer of Waiting

I wait before you like an embarrassed child, wanting your Word,
yearning to know the way, hoping to be led by you, but so filled
with my own trembling I do not always feel your touch. Each
day I dream my deeds and too often, with clumsy action I mar
them in the doing. Now I gather all the strands of my life
together and hold them up in your presence, waiting for the
Word that will set me free from any shame, the Word that will
send me forth again on the path of your will. You have created
all of us in love and promised to see us through this life. I wait
for the veil to be lifted from my sight that I might behold the
world through your eyes. Amen.

Spiritual Exercises
for
Waiting

1. We spend countless minutes, even hours, of our life waiting. We wait for a bus that is late. We wait in a doctor's office. We wait in grocery checkout lines and traffic jams. This is waiting that is outside of our control—or at least it appears to be. Instead of seeing this time as one of passivity, however, we can be active—spiritually active. Here are two possible ways.

   a. Instead of fuming with impatience as you wait, shift your perception and see this time as a respite from a busy day. Spend a few minutes thinking gentle thoughts: of those you love; of something joyful or fulfilling that has happened to you recently; of your connection with the Infinite and Eternal One. Say a prayer of gratitude inwardly, "Thank you for slowing me down and giving me this time to wait for you, God." Move from impatience into a conscious state of creative waiting.

   b. As you wait in a line, in your mind go down the line of people and silently bless each one. Imagine your blessing releasing the tensions they are feeling, diffusing hurts or animosities. Gradually, what you are giving to others will come back to you.

2. Although we are forced physically to wait for mundane reasons many times a day, we are also waiting for other reasons. We are longing for a career break, more money, for that special someone to love us. Consider such a longing in your life. What are you waiting for? Name this longing in your spiritual journal. Then consider these questions and write your responses.

a. Did I once have what I long for now? If so, where did it go and how did I lose it? Can I recover it?

b. How long have I waited? Is it time for me to let go of that waiting and move on?

c. Would my life be better if what I am longing for would come to me? Or do I have what I need now? What has this waiting taught me, and how can it continue to serve me?

After you have considered these questions, write a letter to God, expressing what you are waiting for and why you want it. Read the letter aloud, giving voice to your longing, releasing its energy into the hands of your Creator. Know that God has listened and will either answer at the time right for you or release you from waiting for something that is not destined to come.

15

Giving

Blessed are those who give compassion to the world,
for they shall burst the bonds of suffering and death.

A new understanding of spirituality is emerging. It used to be
that those who accepted the "higher" call to a contemplative
lifestyle disengaged themselves from the world of sensual, competitive, messy human existence. God was not to be found in the
marketplace but as far from the marketplace as possible. But
today we are beginning to challenge the separation of spirituality and social action. We are beginning to realize that the truly
holy people, the "saints" if you will, are those through whom
the presence and power of God is mediated to the world rather
than those who have forsaken the world.

This link between spirituality and liberation is most clearly
demonstrated in the piety of Latin American Christianity as well

as feminist theology in North America. Maintaining the balance between enlightenment and action is not as easy as it sounds, even though it is essential. Motives behind each have to be examined. The spiritual discipline of giving is expressed not just in what we do with our money—although that is certainly one very important aspect of it—but also to be found in our acts of charity and our deeds of mercy.

John Cheever wrote a short story called "Christmas Is a Sad Season for the Poor." In this story, Charlie is an elevator operator in a posh, high-rise apartment building in New York City. Feeling sorry for himself because he has to work on Christmas Day, he solicits sympathy from the apartment tenants by responding to their greetings of "Merry Christmas" with a sad rejoinder of how difficult Christmas is for a person like himself who lives alone in a furnished room. As the day progresses, he changes his story from the lonely bachelor to the poor father with many children and back again, as his mood changes. His melancholy arouses an outpouring of sympathy from the tenants, which results in fourteen dinners and an avalanche of presents for him and his imaginary children. In addition, he is furnished with every conceivable drink that can be concocted for the holiday occasion.

Charlie gets drunk and starts shooting the elevator up and down the shaft at full speed. When he does this with a terrified Mrs. Gadshill in the elevator, he is fired from his job. Feeling depressed and unworthy, he puts the presents given to his imaginary children in a burlap bag and drags them home to his landlady and her three skinny children. The landlady's children, however, have received so many presents from other charitable agencies that by the time Charlie arrives they are confused with receiving. The landlady wisely realizes her children do not need these presents and decides to take them over to the poor people on Hudson Street, people who are needier than she.

Writes Cheever, "First love, then charity, then a sense of power drove her. She knew that we are bound, one to another, in licentious benevolence for only a single day, and that day was nearly over. She was tired, but she couldn't rest."[1]

Unfortunately, many of us fall into that same trap. We are tired, but we go on trying to perform our acts of charity and deeds of mercy. We are caught in our own need to take care of those whose plight is worse than our own. It somehow solidifies our sense of good and increases our power if we do this.

Once I preached a sermon titled "To the Church of God in Seattle." In this sermon I fantasized what the Apostle Paul might write to us, were he able to do so. Drawing from the loving yet stern correctives he sent to the churches of his own day, I had Paul commend our church for its deeds of charity, such as operating a food bank, a clothing thrift shop and a free lunch program for street people. But Paul reprimanded us for allowing the poverty that necessitates these agencies to exist in the world's wealthiest nation. His suggestion was that the poor serve a useful function for us because they give us an outlet to vent our sincere but often misguided benevolence, instead of using our energies to correct the situations that create and perpetuate poverty.

The sermon drew a voluble and immediate discharge of hostility and outrage from several members in the church who volunteer their time in the food bank, thrift shop or lunch program. They felt I had betrayed them, did not understand them, and was impugning their sincere and noble actions. When I had properly apologized to the offended and tried to assure them that their work was indeed appreciated and that was not what I had intended to convey, we finally settled back into our established positions. The lesson had been misunderstood, and the poor continued to officiate over our need to perform our acts of charity and deeds of kindness.

What is missing in much of our good works is sincere, genuine compassion. Henri Nouwen points out that compassion is derived from the Latin words *pati* and *cum*, which together mean "to suffer with." True compassion, he says, asks us to go where it hurts; to enter into places of pain; to share in brokenness, fear, confusion and anguish; to be weak with the weak and powerless with the powerless. This kind of compassion requires more than a general sort of kindness or act of well-doing. It requires putting ourselves in the shoes of the needy and walking in the direction of collective solutions to end their suffering.[2]

Most of us are skeptical of such a compassion. We see it as masochistic or unrealistic. We are all appreciative of the late Mother Teresa and her Missionaries of Charity, who go about the world serving the poorest of the poor. But for the majority, such a life is unattractive, repelling and even disgusting. The less we are confronted with real human suffering, the less we have to deal with it and do anything about it.

Something sinister often lies at the heart of our impulses to do good, and that is, as Nouwen suggests, a sense of competition. We are trained in this world to be competitive rather than compassionate. Even our national gestures of compassion are generated more by the politics of competition than genuine, sincere caring. This is no reason to stop the help. It is only analyzing it for what it is.

Many First World Christians see an incompatibility between political/economic liberation and spirituality. That is because in the past Christians involved themselves in withdrawal from the world rather than engagement in it. Even the contemplative lifestyle often served as an escape from the needs and pains of the world. Today we know better. We are beginning to realize that spirituality calls us to be fully aware of the world in which we live, to be present in it with all its needs and pains, to serve it with compassionate action, and to see more clearly than ever before the systemic reasons for poverty and need. This is what made Mother Teresa the great figure of compassion that she was—she knew that she had been called to follow Jesus into the valley of tears and suffering, to serve a portion of humanity that is in agony. Her call grew from her own life of prayer and spiritual devotion.

We are not all called to work with the poorest of the poor. Mother Teresa would be the first to avow that. However, we are all called to be compassionate, whether we follow Jesus or not, and from that call comes our vocation, the work we are to do, where and with whom we do it.

It would be naive to assume that everyone has the contemplative temperament. Some of us are strong social activists. Others are more comfortable with academic pursuits. The spiritual disciplines have never appealed to the masses, partially because not everyone has the temperamental bent that makes the contemplative life appealing and natural. But recognizing these individual differences does not cancel out the possibility of all of us sharing in the spiritual enterprise. It only means that we may select different arteries of approach. Whether our religious temperament be mental, social, mystical or sacrificial does not negate the fact that each of us is called to make our home in God, to come to God in simple faith, by earnest repentance and with the kind of prayer that is most natural to us, and to be a compassionate, loving presence in the world.

We also need to be prepared for the fact that our interests and approach will shift at different points in life. There was a time in my own spiritual development when the way of the head seemed to take precedence. This was true during my years of college, seminary training and early ministry. During those years I immersed myself in academic pursuits and scholastic explorations.

Then after a few years in ministry there came a shift. I was catapulted into the social arena as an activist. At that time I was still devoted to the religious life but lazy and sporadic in my devotional disciplines. I was feeling somewhat impatient with the church, what I saw as its dull ceremonies and empty traditions, its inability to effect any social changes, indeed to even care. Literal interpretations of the Bible repelled me and seemed like the shell of the crayfish that hides its meat. Systematic reading of the Bible had become dull, and theological study seemed fruitless.

I tried to quell this spiritual combat by plunging feverishly from the way of the head into the way of the hand. I became involved in actions of protest against discrimination against blacks. I marched against the Vietnam War, I spoke out for homosexual rights, I became an advocate of fair housing and equal employment. In short, I took up nearly every social cause that appeared on my landscape, because I believed that is what a Christian should do. It was a clear case of the social environment (in this case the 1960s) shaping the form of my religion.

At the end of that era I began to feel burned out in all directions. Then I experienced another breakthrough. Books of a mystical nature began to speak to me. Private prayer took on new meaning, and I entered into a new dimension of disciplined silence and listening to God. I reduced my time commitment to the church so I could go back to school and work on a doctorate and chose mysticism in world religions as my focus of study. I became more reflective, inward-looking, soul-searching, contemplative. I had finally been led through the way of the head and the hand to the way of the heart. I had become a mystic, and for the first time, I knew I was coming home.

One thing has become increasingly clear for me since this shift. The human temperament, no matter what particular direction it chooses and feels most comfortable with, is essentially a religious temperament. We have come from God, and we all have a longing and hunger to know God. We have a need to find the way of the heart, at least fully if not exclusively. I believe if we pursue this way with sufficient earnestness, we will be led into an everlasting love for God and a desire to serve God more totally in the world with our hands and head.

What happened to me in that shift was that I became painfully aware of the need for prayer to precede action. I had seen how prayer without action can grow into a kind of powerless pietism, and I had seen how action without prayer can degenerate into sophistic manipulation. Now through contemplative prayer I began to see how effective social action must be a manifestation of God's compassionate presence in the world if it is going to have any lasting effect or spiritual value.

The temptation of activism is known to many of us. This was the temptation that Jesus fought in the wilderness, that the disciples fought on numerous occasions. It is the temptation to give visibility to our own power. But the spiritual life directs us to give visibility not to our own power but to God's compassion. While we may never be able to claim pure motives in everything we do, it is important to recognize the places and times where our personal needs begin to dominate our actions.

"I am not appreciated for what I do" is the common cry in churches among those who are trying to serve God in the social arena. This is usually a clear signal that "what I do," whether it is feeding the hungry, clothing the poor or some other worthwhile activity, is more an expression of one's individual needs than God's compassion. Our needs dominate our actions when we offer our services to someone in this way. We communicate subtly yet powerfully this message: "I have something you don't have; I am now going to give it to you. Then I will be doing my duty, and you will be better off than you are now." Having done that, we look around and wait for praise to be expressed for our good deeds. What this is really saying is that we are involved in competition rather than compassion. We can continue to hold power over the ones who are down by the dole we give out.

Eventually we will become exhausted, burned out and even embittered by such efforts. It happened to me. I have seen it happen to others. When we are primarily concerned about being praised, rewarded or liked, then we have chosen to do those things that we hope will elicit such responses.

One way to avoid the temptation of activism is to remind ourselves from the words of Paul, "I can do all things in Christ, who strengthens me." There is an implication here of more than Christ giving us strength for what we do. There is also an underlying reality that Christ has already done what needs to be done. We are simply following Christ's lead. The work has been accomplished. The kingdom is at hand.

Then why, you ask, are we still surrounded by such chaos, such violence and such hatred? Why is our world more a wilderness than it was a generation ago? I am not sure it is. We have made tremendous strides in all the social arenas. The battle for social and racial equality is not over, but we have made headway. While many blacks in America are better off economically, socially and in every way in our country than they were twenty years ago, we must not overlook the fact that one-third of our nation's 28.6 million blacks (12 percent of our population) still live below the poverty line and are chronically poor and alienated from mainstream society.

In Christ all suffering and deprivation have already been reconciled. Our action must simply be to make visible that which has already been accomplished. We can walk on solid ground, even in this new wilderness, knowing that the wilderness has already been traveled by Christ.

I hope you will not think I am saying there is nothing we need to do. Activism is still very much needed, and prayer that doesn't lead us to engage actively with our wilderness and its problems is prayer misused. I am only saying that our activism must spring from prayer, from contemplation, from God and, yes, from self-knowledge.

Our anxiety to solve social problems usually stems from our lack of self-knowledge. The quality of our work depends decisively on the manner and extent to which we know ourselves. Yet we tackle the big problems of life with only the slenderest knowledge about ourselves. The main content of all religious teaching should be the cultivation of self-knowledge, but it has been sadly lacking in our Westernized version of Christianity. It is this missing element that modern mysticism is trying to replace. Why do I do what I do? Why do I react the way I do? Who am I, and what is my purpose in the world? These questions are rarely confronted at any significant depth before we plunge ourselves madly and feverishly into the morass of trying to offer help to the suffering or redirecting the human race away from the self-destructive course it has started to follow.

We need a confrontation with the wilderness of self, an open, honest engagement with our inner being that will unmask our illusions of power and free us from idolatry of all kinds. We cannot profess a solidarity with the oppressed and suffering peoples of this world if we have no sense of solidarity in ourselves. Self-knowledge will prevent us from becoming alienated from the world as we confront it.

Thomas Merton expressed this understanding when he wrote

> *The world as pure object is something that is not there.*
> *It is not a reality outside us for which we exist. It is a*
> *living and self-creating mystery of which I myself am a*
> *part, to which I am myself my own unique door. When*
> *I find the world in my own ground, it is impossible to*
> *be alienated by it.*[3]

As I have said, our acts of charity and deeds of kindness can be systems of competition or control for us. We are always trying to make things happen, wanting to be in control of our own lives, the lives of those close to us, and endless projects. Until we can accept things as they are, rather than attempting to shape them according to our own desires and needs, we have no hope of bringing about the right changes. I can't recall who said it, but I like this statement: "Creation generously showers her blessings upon us, as long as we don't try to wrest them from her."

We do not need to take life for granted. Neither do we need to labor to make it happen. Life is a miracle, a miracle that can only be fully realized by living through God. Our routines of social and economic patterns sometimes interfere with that miracle, but still, it is life itself that is our best asset. Our deeds in the social arenas need to be adventures in the realm of the spiritual, if indeed our deeds are to bring hope into the sordid and despairing poverty that afflicts many.

The world often demands of us a show of strength. But God asks of us a show of vulnerability. That is why in the spiritual life we are asked only to give ourselves. Our deeds of charity, our gifts and tithes, will automatically follow when we have given ourselves. Our reality is not our strength but our vulnerability. Paul reminds us if we give away all we have but have not love, we have given nothing. We need to find ourselves as one small piece of fragmented humanity, to know that we are no more loved and no better than the person we try to help, before we can work to bring the broken pieces of life back together.

I read of an experiment in the devastated areas of the South Bronx of New York City where $300,000 of public money was used to paste vinyl sheets of decals over the windows of abandoned buildings, showing window shades, flower pots, lace curtains and Venetian blinds. They wanted the buildings to appear lived in, hoping by the illusion to defer vandalism and to cheer those living nearby. "Perception is the reality," remarked New York City's housing commissioner in defense of the project.

Is perception the reality? Is covering up the windows with fake images, to console if not fool the public, the reality? Or is the reality the need to get busy and work seriously on a long-term solution?

We need to rouse ourselves from the torpor that would try to convince us that perception is the reality. Reality is infinitely more difficult to achieve than illusion, and it is a thousand times more valuable. What we see, or think we see, is only a small portion of what is really there. That's why in the area of social activism we need to have our vision cleared and our senses deepened, to watch for ways to enlarge our consciousness and strengthen our compassion. If we patiently persist in this, God will eventually sweep back the curtain of our illusions and permit us to see things as they really are.

Starr Daily writes of a woman whose only son was committed to prison as a psychopathic criminal. The woman's suffering reached the point where her soul seemed to die, as well as her body, mind and spirit.

> *In a dull, aimless state of lingering shock she walked out into her garden one morning and stood looking through half-seeing eyes at a freshly spun spider's web. Suddenly she beheld the ethereal form, or the invisible counterpart of the web. It was indescribably beautiful, radiant, and unbelievably perfect in every filigreed detail. Her inner eyes had opened to leave her breathless and spellbound at this sight she was beholding. She was almost afraid to move even an eyelid, lest the vision vanish, leaving her with the horrible conviction that it was an illusion, a mocking indictment of her tottering mind, swallowing up this joy that was bursting at the seams of her heart and soul.*
>
> *Then, a vision more amazing moved into her sight. The spider came out of its hiding place, clothed in the same luster as its web. It paused at the core of the web and seemed to be studying her. Suddenly the little creature excited a vast love for it in the woman's heart. Impulsively she put her finger up close to the spider, and it walked out of its web and onto her hand. Then everything about her came alive with light—every shrub and tree and flower, and even the blades of grass. In the rapture of her experience her tragedy was nonexistent. In a state of pure bliss, she loved all things with a love she had never dreamed possible for a human being. Her heart seemed to melt in a crucible of gratitude, of thankfulness to God. "I knew that my*

boy was safe in God's loving arms," she affirmed. She heard herself repeating a truth her son had uttered as a child: "God has never made any thing that is bad." [4]

Surely that is the vision we need. God is good. God's love is everywhere present. And everything God has made is essentially and inherently good. That is the conviction that will turn our acts of charity into gifts of spontaneous and unbridled love. Compassionate action is the grateful and joyous response to our encounter with a compassionate God. Compassionate action is the greatest gift we can ever bestow.

A Prayer of Giving

O God, Creator of the Universe and Giver of All Good Gifts, what do I have to give you? I give you my money in some of the same spirit that I offer a coin to a panhandler, hoping to get rid of your troubling spirit in my life. I give my good deeds and kind words to another, thinking that I shall thus fulfill the law and gain a little peace for myself. But all the time, what you want is for me to give myself to you, for if you have me, then you have everything I have, and I have everything you have. I give to you today as much of myself as I can, knowing that the gift is not totally complete, but also knowing that you will give me another opportunity tomorrow, and in due season will bring forth the fruit of your kingdom in my life. By the forgiveness of Christ I dare to pray. Amen.

Spiritual Exercises
for
Giving

These exercises require physical action, while holding to this aphorism: *That which I give to others, I give to myself.*

1. Walk down a street and smile at every person whose eyes meet your own. Keep walking but observe the reactions you receive.

2. Give something to someone who has a greater need than you. How does it make you feel to do this? Are you anxious about how your gift will be used or received? Or are you willing to let go of your gift once it is offered?

3. Make a monetary gift to a charitable organization or an institution whose work you believe in.

4. Give something to the earth or the earth's creatures, something that will bless and not harm in any way.

5. Give something to yourself, something that gives you pleasure, satisfaction and joy.

In your spiritual journal write about each of these giving experiences and answer these questions. What single word embodies all these gifts? Why did I give? If I did not complete all the above exercises, which ones did I skip and why? Which gift was the hardest to give? Which was the easiest? What was given to me as a result of my giving?

16

Forgiving

*Blessed are those who forgive life for
not being all they have wanted it to be,
for they shall create a new beginning for themselves.*

The spiritual discipline of forgiveness is the hardest discipline to live. The litany of forgiveness needed in this world seems endless. The Koreans need to forgive the Japanese, the Jews need to forgive the Germans, the Palestinians need to forgive the Jews, Native and African Americans need to forgive Caucasian Americans. And on it goes. These ancient hatreds and grudges bind us to the pain of the past and prevent us from moving on.

In our personal lives we are constantly being confronted with the necessity of forgiveness. It may be we have to forgive abusive or absent parents, insensitive and domineering teachers, unloyal friends or mates. It is likely we also have to forgive ourselves for moral failures and imperfect performances. It may even be necessary that we learn to forgive God for not giving us a better life or for not intervening and answering our fervent prayers.

How shall we learn to forgive? Where shall we find the guidelines? It is at this level the Bible becomes a valuable resource. The men and women in the Bible are there primarily to help us find ourselves. In their lives, in their struggles between giving in to their lower instincts or being obedient to God, we see ourselves and our struggle and slowly begin to awaken to the truth of our own being.

The story of Joseph, as it is told us in the Book of Genesis, is a story of forgiveness. Joseph was a younger son of a rather prosperous farmer named Jacob. Jacob had twelve sons, and while Joseph was regarded with great fondness by his father, his older brothers looked upon him as an unwelcome afterthought. A tragic triangle is set in place in this story among the one who loves too much (Jacob), those who feel loved too little (the brothers), and the one who is loved too much (Joseph). This triangle represents the human tragedy and sets in motion the need for forgiveness.

One night pampered little Joseph had a dream in which the sheaves of wheat belonging to his brothers bowed down to the sheaf of wheat belonging to Joseph. This was followed by another dream in which the sun, moon and eleven stars (representing his eleven brothers) also bowed down to him. Joseph unwisely reported his dreams to his brothers, and this only stirred their hatred more deeply. They concluded that the way to get rid of the dreams was to get rid of the dreamer. So one day they stripped him of his beautiful robe with the long sleeves and sold him as a slave to a passing caravan of Ishmaelites, which was going into Egypt. The brothers then told their father a wild beast had killed Joseph. They showed him Joseph's robe, which they had dipped in the blood of a goat. Jacob was heartbroken over the loss of his favorite son.

In Egypt, Joseph was purchased by an Egyptian named Potiphar, one of the Pharoah's court officials. So Joseph began a new life as a slave in a royal household. He quickly rose through the ranks and eventually into the service of the Pharaoh, ranking second only to the king himself.

Then came a series of crop failures followed by a great famine. Joseph had prudently caused huge quantities of grain to be stored for such an occasion, so that "the whole world came to Egypt to buy grain from Joseph, so severe was the famine everywhere" (Genesis 41:57).

Meanwhile, back at the ranch in Canaan, Jacob and his family were suffering hard times, so he sent his sons into Egypt to purchase grain. Joseph recognized his brothers, but they did not know him. He pretended harshness at first, accusing them of being spies and causing them to be thrown into prison for three days. Then he said he would release them and send them home with some grain, but they must return with the youngest son, Benjamin, as proof that they were not spies. He kept one of the brothers as hostage until their return. Joseph was struggling between resentment and love.

The brothers returned to their father and discovered, on opening their sacks of grain, that the silver they had given for its purchase had been replaced in their sacks. Frightened and confused, they told their father what had happened and that they must return to Egypt with young Benjamin. At first Jacob refused, for he was still grieving over the loss of his son Joseph. But the famine became more severe, and finally he was forced to send his sons back to Egypt for more grain, this time allowing Benjamin to accompany them.

At his second meeting with his brothers, Joseph learned his

father was still alive. He could no longer keep his identity secret. Through his tears he told them who he was and assured them they need not be distressed or blame themselves for what they did, for through their act of betrayal many lives had been saved from starvation. He then kissed each of his brothers and invited them to go home and bring their father back to live near him, so they could all be together again. Joseph and his father are finally reunited. Jacob begged Joseph to forgive his brothers' crime and wickedness, even though they had done him great harm. Joseph assured Jacob and his brothers he had forgiven all of them and said again, "You meant to do me great harm; but God meant to bring good out of it by preserving the lives of many people. Do not be afraid, I will always provide for you" (Genesis 50:20–21).

So ends one of the most touching stories in human literature. While it is a story of a father and his grief, of brothers and their jealousy, it is supremely a story of forgiveness. And it is also our story. We are all children of grief—the grief of empty failure, of dreams unfulfilled, of tomorrows crushed by the harshness and betrayal of today, of death destroying our highest hopes or robbing us of our dearest love.

But we can be more than that. We can be more than the grief-stricken father or the shortsighted brothers. We can also be Joseph, the one who determines to meet the world with kindness, no matter how harshly it greets him. A naive and guileless child becomes a noble and compassionate adult, who is neither intimidated by a ruthless king nor seduced by a calculating woman. Nor does he allow himself to become bitter over an unkind past or an unsympathetic family. Instead he sees the purpose of God moving through all the events of his life. He even sees himself fulfilling part of God's universal desire for good, in spite of and ultimately because of every human effort to do evil. So in the end, it is God who is at work in this story. The only thing the characters have to do is to forgive.

The theme of forgiveness is paramount in Jesus' teachings, particularly in his Sermon on the Mount. In Luke's version of this sermon, we are reminded that "God is kind to the ungrateful and the selfish" (Luke 6:35). Grace and forgiveness find their reason in God and not in the nature of humans, those who are the recipients of grace and forgiveness. Jesus told his followers that the way to avoid being a victim was to take charge of their lives and their situations by taking the initiative in loving, caring and giving. Do this, he said, expecting nothing in return from anyone except God, "for the measure you give will be the measure you get back."

That which we give to others, we also give to ourselves. When we forgive, we receive the grace of forgiveness back into our own lives, for as the imperfect departs from our lives, the perfect begins its struggle to return. Forgiveness puts an end to our suffering and anger and changes our world to a place of joy, abundance, love and endless giving. And thus the journey, which we began as sons and daughters of God, ends in the light from which we all came.

Forgiveness, as I see it, is a three-pronged affair. We have to forgive others, we have to forgive ourselves, and we have to forgive God. In the process we will forgive our world for being less than a perfect place, and we will learn to love it and all that is in it, including ourselves, with something of the unconditional and universal love of our Heavenly Parent God. Although forgiveness may be the most difficult belief we have to live with, in the end it becomes our most vital endeavor, for out of it comes our fullest life. Only as we love ourselves and each other can we begin to love God. Then we can see, as did Joseph, that everything in life can be redemptive.

I have stated that forgiveness is a three-pronged affair. Let's examine each of these prongs now, for each is necessary if we are to truly live forgiveness.

1. *Forgiving others* is often looked upon as the full work of forgiveness, but I say it is the place where we start the process. Trained as we are to look outside ourselves for what is wrong, we have to forgive what we see "out there" before we can learn to forgive what is wrong within us. We all know people who don't care, who are unconscious and have no idea that what they say or do is hurtful to others. We have to forgive them in the same way and for the same reason that Jesus forgave those who placed him on the cross, because "they know not what they do."

We also have to forgive the monsters of the world, those who do such evils as ordinary people dare not dream of. A close examination of their lives will generally reveal to us that at an early stage in life these monsters were themselves severely and tragically victimized. It may also show us the presence of a psychopathic mentality, a mental illness of tragic proportions. They wound others because they are deeply wounded.

Why forgive them? We don't forgive because it will reduce the evil in our world. We don't even forgive them because it will reduce the evil in their own lives. It may do neither. We forgive them to reduce the evil within ourselves. We are the ones who suffer most when we refuse to forgive another. The hatred and resentment within us, if harbored and nurtured, can actually become toxic and over a period of time will cause physical or mental deterioration in us. Lewis Smedes says there are four stages through which we pass when we forgive: we hurt, we hate, we heal and we come together again.[1]

The story of Joseph follows this pattern, leaving us with a

feeling of satisfaction at seeing this family reunited. But the fact is that forgiveness does not always bring us together again. An abused wife may learn to forgive her husband, but that does not necessarily mean they will be reconciled. Unless he admits his problem and is willing to work on it, they should never be together again.

My major work of forgiveness came with my father, but it did not begin until after he was dead. I had a litany of reasons for feeling resentful toward him. If he had been a better provider for us, my mother would not have left him. If he had not insisted on hiding himself away in his mountain retreat and looking for the bonanza that forever eluded him, he could have given us financial support. If he had been of stronger moral fiber, he would not have succumbed to drinking, dying eventually from cirrhosis, the common disease of alcoholics. We can always find reasons to verify our resentments, but we can never find the reason that will support clinging to resentment of any kind. Besides, the list of reasons we may create are always seen from our biased point of view, giving no recognition or sympathy for the reasons by which the other person may have been forced to live.

I was in college when my father died. When I received the telegram informing me of his death in Salt Lake City and requesting that I come at once, I began to think of excuses that would prevent me from going. Chief among them was money. I was working to put myself through college, since my father could not give me any financial support and my stepfather would not. But even as the excuses mounted, some inner wisdom whispered, "You must go."

Each event has its own way of educating us into the nature of things. It is perhaps easier to be in the position of the victim than to be the person conscious of his or her responsibilities and of the gifts by which we are endowed. But the latter is the only way to inner maturity. Every loss and grief are ways to gain Self. My sense of being excluded by my father sprang from my being out of touch with me, that part known as the higher self, or the final me. The Indian poet and saint Kabir sums up what I am trying to describe: "If thy soul is a stranger to thee, the whole world becomes unfriendly." Forgiveness springs from the soul, whereas resentment grows from the mind. The soul will often override the reasoning power of the mind. Had I not gone to my father's funeral, I don't think I would have done the necessary work of forgiveness, at least not at that time.

The moment of seeing my father in his coffin was singular. What I remember most from that moment was seeing his hands. They were strong hands, even though somewhat gnarled and roughened from years of swinging a miner's pick. Although the mortician had arranged them clasped in front to give the appearance of serene rest, strength and labor still clung to those hands. I wept then for the first time, not just over his death but over the wasted, empty years of our lives. I wept because it was too late to say I loved and forgave him for everything I might have perceived as neglect. For in truth, he had given much and had done the very best he could.

Everyone does. We do the best we can. If we knew a better way, we would do it. From a critical point of view, we can make our judgments and assessments, but from a soul level, there are no judgments. Only understanding and love.

My father came to me one night in a dream. He stood at my bedside and placed his hands on my head. I awoke with a sense of peace that our relationship was being healed and that his lonely life was being fulfilled. I awoke knowing I had not only forgiven him, I had also forgiven myself.

2. *Forgiving ourselves* takes more courage because it requires greater honesty. We have all hurt ourselves at some time or place, unfairly and sometimes deeply. Whenever we hurt someone else, we hurt ourselves, whether we know it or not. The unfair harm we did to others is usually the hardest to forgive, particularly when we cannot make amends. The time we lied to someone who trusted us, turned away from someone who needed us, demeaned someone who was weaker and did not deserve it, condemned another by our own projections—these are some of the little acts that can keep us from feeling at one with ourselves. The pain we cause other people often turns into the hate we feel for ourselves.

Unfortunately, we judge, convict and sentence ourselves for our wrongdoing in a secret, almost passive way. Sometimes we don't even know what we are doing to ourselves, and yet we lack the energy to bless ourselves, to feel proud of our accomplishments, or to feel glad for just being alive. I think one of the root causes of depression is lack of self-forgiveness.

The only way we can ever be whole again is to have the courage and honesty to look at all our failures and deceptions and forgive ourselves. We did the best we could. If we had known a better way, we would have done it. Now we have found a better way, the way of forgiveness, and it is by forgiving ourselves that we find the freedom and the will to bless ourselves and to move forward joyously into life's next adventure.

We have to stop moving toward God for the purpose of protection, consolation or even forgiveness. We do not go to God to address questions of justification or to make requests of any kind. We go simply *to behold and to be held*. To behold and to be held. In that process we will change. We will change from separated creatures who are angry at others or themselves into persons who want to link up with the whole. While our asking forgiveness of God is important to us, in that it places us vulnerable and honest before God, it is not our asking that brings it. It is our willingness to receive God more deeply into our lives, for the very nature of God is forgiveness.

An ancient principle of the Tao tells us that everything is right and in harmony just as it is. Such a principle is logically nonsensical. But when we have had the unexpected experience of having our world quietly transfigured by forgiveness, then we see everything as perfectly interconnected with everything else, so that nothing is irrelevant or nonessential, because everything is of God.

3. *Forgiving God* is made even more difficult by the affirmation that everything is of God. Most of us think it is audacious and sinful to imagine that we would ever need to forgive God for anything. Yet buried deep inside is often a sense of anger against God for not doing something about the bad things that are in this world and over which we seem to have little control. Although it may seem a sacrilege to wrestle with God (Chapter 13), it may appear to be an even greater one to talk about forgiving God. How dare we, mortal creatures that we are, hold any kind of grudge or resentment against our Immortal Creator! The "bloody yet unbowed head" must somehow be lowered in deference to the inscrutable ways of a tyrannical God, or so we were taught by our Augustinian and Calvinist precursors. And if we can't stomach that kind of theology, then we can get out of the church. Which is precisely what many have done. Who can live with a God that refuses even our anger?

Sometimes under the incredible force of suffering and death, the only way we can accept the notion that life has limitations is initially through anger. When the full force of suffering strikes us, when we confront the fact that God, to whom we have ascribed omnipotence, does nothing to alleviate the world's pain, we may have to linger with the mystery of the disorders of life before we can even begin to grasp the reality of grace. A father I knew placed his little son, who had not yet learned to walk, in a jump swing. The child accidentally got caught in the harness of the swing and strangled before the father realized what was happening. Filled with the deepest guilt, remorse and rage he had ever known, the father said to me, "How easy it would have been for God to untangle that strap, yet he did nothing. I don't think I trust God anymore."

That's how we all feel at one time or another until we begin to learn some new things about God. There are certain things God can do and will do. God will give us the kind of world we want without interfering. But there are also things that God cannot or will not do. God will not abrogate that precious and often painful gift of human freedom given to us on our day of creation, no matter how unwisely or harmfully we choose to exercise it. In other words, God is limited by the God-imposed laws of this universe.

The one thing God does with all of us is to suffer with us when we suffer and to forgive us continually, even when we are struggling with our anger against God. We do not see the whole picture of what God is doing, and we have only meager scraps of information as to what God really is. To blame God for the evil that seems to go unchecked in the world, despite our fervent and beseeching prayers, is to miss the whole point. We grow only by "enlarging the place of our tent," while remaining centered in a demanding and illuminating faith in an ordered universe. We have no choice but to live in the midst of all our tasks, questions, successes and failures, experiences and bewilderments, and to throw ourselves utterly into the arms of God. We come to God to behold life, not directing our thoughts to our own suffering but to the suffering of God in the world. And God will hold us and help us to be more deeply rooted in this life. *To behold and to be held.* This is what we receive when we come to God, no matter what weary turning point has directed us there.

Christianity is the only religion in the world that asks us to forgive our enemies, no matter what they have done and no matter who they may be. If God has become our enemy, then it is God we need to forgive before we can move on with our work.

Someone has said that forgiveness is the determination to keep all our human options open. I like that. I also think forgiveness is the determination to accept our divine options, whatever they may be. Forgiveness opens us to the possibility of being illuminated by God's grace, of receiving the gift of insight that is not our own but that comes from the Divine Other in our lives.

To be forgiven is not necessarily having the slate wiped clean. It is having Someone there who lives with us, dirty slate and all. This Someone, whether the divine grace in another person or divine grace from an infinite source, leaves all the options of love open, right down to loving the person in ourselves that does the very same thing to others that has been done to us. A woman, participating in a workshop on human relationships, said, referring to the behavior of another person, "I must learn to love the person in me who does the very same thing." Relationships, wherever they may be formed and carried out, are very fragile. There is always something to forgive if the relationship is to continue. The will to forgive and the willingness to be forgiven are the only means by which relationships can be sustained.

Healing and forgiveness are somehow tied in together. One doesn't happen without the other. The heart suffocates, cries out and wants to escape its pain. Its cry mobilizes the visible and invisible powers in the universe, and as we learn to forgive whatever or whoever has caused our pain, we are healed and walk the earth again as the word made flesh.

I remember as a child walking along the meadow pasture that framed the Little Lost River, taking delight in the plaintive song of a killdeer, that tiny bird who is so named because the cry it makes sounds strangely like "kill-dee." Then a strange thing happened. Instead of flying away, as it had first been doing, the bird suddenly flew in front of me, dropped to the ground and began to drag itself along as though it had a broken wing. I followed it for some distance, crawling softly on my hands and knees through the meadow grass. Sometimes I would seem so near that I could touch it. At one point it seemed I looked into its eyes. Yet it always seemed to keep ahead of me, just out of my reach.

I cannot remember how long we kept at this little game. Once when I tired of it and stopped, the bird came back toward me, crying insistently and again dragging a wing along the ground, until I started to follow. Finally, it suddenly rose into the air and, with a final and shrill "kill-dee," was gone, leaving me standing quietly, though sadly, at the edge of the meadow.

In a sense I have been standing there ever since. Nearly half a century later I seem to be hearing the killdeer's song more and more, luring me away from its nest as the intruder when my only wish was to be the visitor. I find myself often on my knees in the grass, following whatever it is that can never be told, yet always felt—the forgiving force that makes life possible.

Forgiveness happens whenever we struggle out of a place of darkness and misunderstanding, to walk, however unsure, in the

light. Forgiveness knows no season. It can be born in us on the
wing of some old song from our childhood. Ultimately, everything is a metaphor, a seduction through an open meadow in
search of the hidden song of a bird. And that search is both our
joy and our hope, just as the search to forgive and be forgiven is
our hope and our joy. Someday we shall be fully found, fully
forgiven and fully restored. Until then, we either search for the
hidden God in the familiar meadow or the unfamiliar
wilderness. Or we learn that it is not in wandering we find God,
but in standing still.

A Prayer of Forgiving

Loving One, in peace and light you created us. In peace and light I now offer forgiveness to those who may have temporarily taken that peace from me or robbed me of some of that light. I forgive myself for not always being true to the best I know. There are many days when the burdens I carry seem to chafe my shoulders and weigh me down, when the road seems dreary and endless, the skies gray and threatening, when my life has no music, and my heart has lost its courage. I forgive those times and ask that you flood my path with light, turn my eyes to skies full of promise, tune my heart to brave music, and so quicken my spirit that I may be able to encourage the souls of others who journey with me on this road of life. Amen.

Why Should I Forgive You?

Why should I forgive you? Because I have seen with my own eyes how the painful flow of life is reversed when people can forgive each other. The harmful, destructive patterns of infidelity, abuse and mistreatment are changed just often enough to make me believe that forgiveness helps reverse the flow of pain and create a place of healing for those who either caused the pain or suffered from it.

Why should I forgive you? It is one way I can heal myself. Even if I had never seen forgiveness change a situation, I would still forgive you, because it is the only way I can heal myself.

Why should I forgive you? I believe forgiveness is as close to God's divine act of creation as I can ever get, for in forgiveness I create a new beginning out of some past pain that should never have existed in the first place. Then I can look at my world and say with God, "It is good."

Why should I forgive you? Because I know you did the best you could. If you had known a better way, you would have done better. When I forgive you, I walk in stride with God, whose very nature is forgiveness, and whose highest will is for both of us to be healed of the hurts we do not deserve.

Why should I forgive you? When I can forgive you, or myself, or God, for any hurt that was undeserved, I find the healing and the wholeness that makes life not only bearable but joyous again. In forgiveness I exchange sickness for wholeness and death for life.

That's why I forgive you, not only today but every day, and in every needed way. I forgive you because forgiveness creates a new heaven and earth for all of us and helps us live in joy and peace again.

Spiritual Exercises
for
Forgiving

This exercise on forgiveness invites you to wrestle over your response to a life situation. Record your thoughts and emotions in your journal as you work through this exercise.

Your friend Jean confides in you that when she was a young girl she was sexually abused by a priest. She tried once to tell her mother, but her mother refused to believe her. Jean grew up and became sexually promiscuous and chemically dependent, until she finally sought help. After several years of treatment, she could acknowledge what had happened and know she was not to blame. She then felt the need to confront the priest. Since he was no longer at the parish, she met with another priest and told him of the abuse she had experienced. He advised her to forgive the priest who had allegedly abused her and move forward with her life. Jean did not feel she had been heard or believed. She returned to her therapist, who was adamant that Jean, who had been a victim, did not need to further victimize herself by forgiving the priest who had robbed her of her childhood innocence. She encouraged Jean to let go of the anger and hurt she had around the incident but not to take on the heavier burden of exonerating the priest.

Jean turns to you with some hard questions. Write your answers in your journal. Does the victim have a responsibility to forgive the victimizer? Where is the justice in this situation? Does forgiveness mean more than exonerating persons from blame? Does it also mean forgiving life when it has failed us, forgiving God who did not protect us?

There are no easy answers when it comes to forgiveness. We are sometimes torn between how we *really* feel versus how we think we *should* feel. Write your definition of forgiveness. Can you live this principle in your life as you look at the hurts, small or big, that you have experienced?

17

Accepting

Blessed are those who accept *every person as holy and who do not burden anyone with narrow judgements or stifled love, for they shall point to that mysterious road that leads back to God.*

My window is open to let the summer morning in. My cat sees this as an invitation to share the wealth, and with a croaking kind of meow, springs in and lays a rumpled and freshly dead mouse on my desk. I am told cats do this because they realize we humans are such poor hunters that we cannot catch our own mice. That may be right, but I am not accepting this trophy from her morning romp. I scoop it up and carry it outside for a decent burial, a procedure she watches with wonderment. She can no more comprehend this strange use of her gift than I can comprehend her cruel delight in torturing the mice, mole and small bird population to death. I am not much attached to rodents, but I am inclined to sign a truce and allow them to live where they wish, as long as it's not in my house or garden. As for birds, I like nothing better than to watch them and would do everything in my power to protect them. Not so with my feline companion. She has no such commitments and makes no such compromises.

This long-haired orange and gray cat, extraordinarily sweet in disposition and affectionately dubbed Orange Roughy, is a patient and usually successful hunter. I have watched her sit motionless for hours, staring at the bank that slopes from our lawn down toward the sea, waiting for the slightest stirring of life in the long grass before she pounces. She accepts her defeats as gracefully as her triumphs. They are each part of the same piece. I am not always so inclined. Would that I were, for my soul tells me that we learn to live fully in the measure in which we learn to live acceptingly.

I used to think of acceptance as the privilege of those who do not have the wisdom to be discerning. Now I think of acceptance as the virtue of those who give to each enterprise and each person as much value as each is capable of taking. Giving and taking, playing and working, meaning and purpose are perfectly balanced in what we call acceptance. I pray for it in the words and spirit of the old prayer, attributed to Neibuhr, that asks for the courage to change what needs to be changed, the serenity to accept what cannot be changed, and the wisdom to know the difference.

I believe that God has a Master Plan for each life. I also believe that my responsibility is to accept that Plan with what Glenn Clark called "divine acquiescence." In that plan God moves people in and out of each other's lives, and each leaves a mark on the other. You find that you are made up of a little bit of every life that has ever touched yours, and you are more because of it and would be less if they had not touched you.

Some people touch your life with love or carelessness and move on. Some touch your life in such a way that when they leave, you breathe a sigh of relief and wonder why you ever came into contact with them. Others leave you, and you breathe a sigh of remorse, while wondering why they had to go away and leave such an empty hole in your life. You look at this coming and going with a kind of wonderment. Children leave their parents. Mates or partners grow apart and leave each other. Friends love and move on. Enemies hate and move on. Think of the many who have moved in your life, some of them living now only in hazy memory.

I think of my grandparents, my father, Mrs. Greenbush, Patricia Lee, my stepfather, Robert and Dwight, two young men that you will meet shortly—all of them gone now, existing only in my memory. I look at the present with wonder and humility. I realize it is futile to question, to regret. I can only accept the Plan and the various ways by which the touch of others on my life helped fulfill the Plan.

My oldest brother's son, Jeff, was killed when he was sixteen. A truck plowed into his motorcycle on a lonely farm road north of Arco, and in a moment his life was over. His family was broken, but they went on, never the same as they were, but going on. It pays to have a faith. Either the world is developing through good and bad chances, as Pierre Teilhard de Chardin suggests, in which case we must serve and love it; or it is simply absurd and cruel, which means we must reject it as much as we can. Faith helps us choose the alternative of acceptance. We go on, trying to perceive what God has in mind, how we should correct our world view, choosing life even though we are surrounded by death.

Besides, things are not always what they appear. As one grows older, it becomes more and more obvious that people and things are like sparks forming on the back of a fireplace, flaring brightly for a time, then transforming into something else. I look at my hands that take the words handed to them by my mind and transpose them onto the page and realize these are the same hands I have always had. Yet they are not the same at all. The skin has begun to lose its elastin, little brown spots have marched across my knuckles, the lines in my palms are deeper and more certain. When did it all happen? There was never a moment when it was not happening. There is nothing to do but accept the drift of this mystery we call aging, to let it have its place and not always be turning up one's soil with the plow of self-examination or regret.

As we age we find that we are more alive than we were when we were younger. In our youth we were caught in absurdly small events and beliefs, dealing with all of them with a small and rigid personality. Then our shell began to crack and we began to stretch and expand until we finally arrived at the larger place of acceptance. We sank down to some deeper level and discovered a fresh supply of life that astounded us and an accepting spirit that delighted us. A part of us remained untouched, inviolate and serene through all this change, knowing that the time would come when we would realize there is more to us than age. Yet it is age that helps us get to that place of full acceptance.

Can it come to us when we are younger? I think it can, at least in measure. But age is the ultimate adventure of the spirit, the fulfillment of the promise that the best is yet to be, and the dawning awareness of the circles in which our souls wish to participate. To deny old age its advantages is to miss the greatest opportunity for growing. "Lamed but not tired," is how one of my senior friends described herself. It was her belief that we should be more concerned about refusing to grow old than about the aging process itself. There are discoveries to be made on every turn of the road and a deeper experience of God is made possible as one's emotions somehow are refined and enlarged. But if we continue to cling to our youth and devote all our energies to a denial of maturity in our bodies, then our spirits will remain juvenile and rigid. I am not demeaning the state of youth. Thank God for it. But acceptance, at its deepest and most sincere levels, is a gift of the years, one of the fringe benefits of age. That is not to say, however, that all older people are accepting. There are tragic examples to the contrary. James Fowler in his definitive work on faith development agrees that adults can get stuck at some lower level of faith and stay there for life. Scott Peck in his four stages of the spiritual journey notes that not all adults arrive at the final level of development but often stop at conventional or authoritarian levels rather than pushing on to a universal faith where love and acceptance are what counts.

Look, for example, at the subject of homosexuality, the big issue for the Christian church as this century draws to a close and one where older people struggle more severely than younger. Can we even talk about homosexuality? About homophobia? Can we listen to differing voices? Sadly, in most churches the dialogue is closed, not only on homosexuality but on sexuality itself. How do we sort through the maze of issues, values and conflicting personal, religious and social concerns surrounding sexuality in general and homosexuality in particular? A major stumbling block to open and productive discussion is the tangled maze of issues and the defensive, polarized reactions of individuals. This psychological and spiritual gridlock makes rational discussion difficult and agreement impossible.

Because this subject impinges so strongly upon the spiritual discipline of acceptance, I want to spend a considerable length of time on it. You, the reader, may have serious disagreement with my conclusions, but I hope you will stay with me, to the end that we might at least agree on what the Christlike response should be to homosexual persons.

Since the fourth century A.D. the church has done little in the area of sexuality except remind us of its dangers. The Western church seems basically regretful that we humans are sexual, sensual creatures and has acted on the wish that sexuality would just go away so we could get on with matters of faith and spirituality. But the time for moralizing and reprisal are over. We now are being forced to deal with sexual issues and to ask ourselves whether sexuality is in fact a gift. Denial of our sexuality is at some level a rejection of God's goodness in giving us this gift in the first place.

The Christian church has constructed most of the codes of sexual behavior that plague us today, telling us what is right and wrong about sex. But if we could drop those outer rules, which haven't really worked, we would be free to seek the law within our own being, which ever directs us to be humane, loving, kind and spontaneous. We would see sexuality as our ally rather than our enemy, giving us an opportunity to better understand ourselves. In seeing it as both gift and friend, we would be able to let it take us back to the Source from which it came in the first place.

Sexual energy was never meant to stop at the level of gratification. If we determine we want to use our sexuality wisely on all levels, we will have to listen and pay attention to what is happening inside of us. In accepting sexuality as God's gift, we will not have to feel separated from that part of ourselves any longer. Remember, God did not give us the gift with a whole set of rules attached. The rules and restrictions were made up by human beings, most of whom did not feel free in their sexual expression and who felt sex was a part of one's baser nature.

What would be the point of God giving us our lives and our sexuality and then laying it all out according to a script? Once we can accept our entire life, including our sexuality, as a gift from God, we can begin to search out the wisest use of this gift, instead of letting it deteriorate into furtive excesses and harmful exploitation of ourselves and others. Life is an amazingly wonder-filled gift that is ongoing, and our sexuality, at its highest levels, is just one more avenue that will help us come Home.

But what about those people, the 10 percent or so of our population, male and female, who express their sexuality with members of the same gender? That population has remained proportionately the same in every culture since as far back as we know. In some cultures, it has been viewed as natural, but by and large the Western world has developed a strong conscious objection to homosexuality, even to the point of classifying it as criminal. Fortunately, changing social mores and religious practices have loosened some of the old taboos and boundaries on sexual behavior, and homosexuality as a lifestyle has been both decriminalized and removed by the American Psychiatric Association in 1973 from their list of mental disorders. Scientific research is now clearly proving the presence of distinctive hormonal and genetic factors in the homosexual male, pointing to evidence for it being biological, something over which the individual has no choice.

If, however, it were scientifically proved beyond any doubt that there is a genetic predisposition toward homosexuality, it would not serve as a compelling moral argument for acceptance. Race is obviously genetic, yet that has not prevented racism and the ugly discrimination that goes with it. Acceptance on a spiritual level must rise out of a spiritual reality that acknowledges that every human being on this earth is a precious and valuable gift, one to be treated with reverence and respect. Sexuality is not a lifestyle. It is a gift from God. When two people form a loving, committed relationship with each other, we should celebrate and affirm it openly, as an expression of God's highest intent.

Homosexuality holds a curious threat over our predominately heterosexual society because it threatens religious rules, cultural values, and gender roles. Some have seen a connection between acceptance of homosexuality and the erosion of the family pattern of male/female bonding, procreation and child rearing. Hence, in the presidential campaign of 1992 the Republicans built a major plank in their platform called "family values," a subtle but direct refutation of the growing legal status of homosexuality. At the same time, nearly every major Christian denomination in this country voted resolutions disallowing ordination of gays or lesbians and denying the validity of same-sex marriages (usually called partnerships). Homosexuality was soundly trounced by religious and political groups that year, with more to follow. Scriptures were usually cited, at least by the conservatives, for support, but for the most part it was a movement based on fear that the traditional unit of society, the family, was being destroyed.

To be fair, it should be noted that not everyone in the political and religious structures of this country has moved in this regressive direction. Fires of acceptance have been steadily stoked by significant numbers of persons and groups, indicating that we are witnessing a major shift in human consciousness. Humanity does not move easily into new paradigms. Acceptance is as great a threat to many as rejection. Hence, the threatened often make a "Custer's Last Stand" to eliminate the forces demanding change.

For many "love" has become a code word for avoiding confrontation or disagreement. For others it is a way to avoid being nice, as expressed in the saw, "love the sinner but hate the sin" (translation: "love the homosexual but hate homosexuality"). The result is that we use love as a means of avoiding acceptance. In the name of loving each other we often do everything we can to diffuse the essence of another. In the name of love we do our labeling, maintain our rigid beliefs, avoid or deny relevant emotional attitudes, and hide our own hidden experiences of shame, fear, guilt or anger. In the name of love we often do everything but accept.

In 1991 the national meeting of American Baptists was held in Charleston, West Virginia. Prior to that meeting, West Virginia Baptists had proposed a resolution that would condemn homosexuality as a lifestyle incompatible with Christian teaching. On the morning that the resolution was to be considered by the delegates in attendance, the call went out to all Baptists from the surrounding area to come to the meeting and vote. There was nothing illegal about this, but had the convention been held in a more liberal area, the resolution might have failed. As it was, it was voted in, causing polarization all across the denomination.

I remember standing outside the convention hall the morning the buses came rolling in with their potential voters. A woman, somewhere in her middle years, crawled down from one of the buses carrying a huge, worn Bible in one hand, while with the other hand she was tugging at the skirt of her nylon dress that had somehow hiked itself up into the crack of her rather generous posterior. She giggled as she finally freed the dress and said to the woman behind her, "Hurry up now, Edna. We gotta git in thar and vote down those homos oncet and fer all."

There would have been something amusing about the spectacle if it had not been so tragic. That large Bible in her hand was antipathetic to all she had come there to do. Where in God's word are we ever allowed the luxury of voting anyone down once and for all, stripping them of their rights and dignity and removing from them every shred of respectability and legitimacy because of the irrefutable fact of their birth?

The religious right has deviously skewed the view of the Scripture in regard to homosexuality. Since I devoted a chapter in my third book, *Love Without Conditions*, to the various biblical citations customarily invoked as relating to homosexuality, I will not do that here. I will remind you, however, that there is no mention of homosexuality in the four Gospels of the New Testament and that Jesus had nothing at all to say on the subject. And I would also argue that the few scriptures that exist in the Old Testament and the writings of Paul are often interpreted incorrectly. The hatemongers and stormtroopers who are out to get the "homos" today read the Bible through the lens of their own personal values and prejudices rather than trying to interpret it with intelligence and honesty.

Hatred of the homosexual has become the last respectable prejudice of our century, with movements afoot now in several states to deny homosexuals the protection of civil rights laws. Some ministers have avowed that homosexuals represent the devil and quote scriptures to prove it. They do not, however, quote the scriptures that talk about the sin of greed, the burdens of wealth, the wrongness of judging, and the imperatives to love all people as God does. In that sense, religious fundamentalism has become dangerous because it refuses to accept diversity and is ruthlessly intolerant and destructive against anything or anyone it cannot convert. Instead of encouraging people to act from love, religious fundamentalism encourages them to act upon their fears. Good people have been deluded by this practice, and good people are being hurt every day as they become the victims of this campaign of hatred and prejudice.

Someday, I believe, the Christian Church will look back in horror and shame at the way it has maligned and persecuted innocent people. The action of the church in this last decade of the twentieth century has been both a scandal and a disgrace and directly refutes the teachings and spirit of Jesus. Even though scriptural support is cited, incorrectly, as a means of legitimizing this persecution, the truth is that a large portion of the collective spirit of Christianity remains unredeemed and opposed to the way of God's universal and all-inclusive love.

One of the best ways to stop our persecution of groups is to begin to know them as individuals. To that end, let me introduce you to Robert, a gay man in my church, who has probably taught me more about loving in the face of hatred than almost anyone I know.

Robert was born in Texas to a strong Southern Baptist family. He was the third of four children and grew up immersed in Baptist mores and culture. He won awards for perfect attendance and Bible verses committed to memory and was often told he should someday be a minister. But Robert had a secret. By the time he was twelve, he knew he was gay. He carried the secret through high school, at which point he felt he needed to tell his family. The information was not welcomed. His father told him he would have to leave home if he persisted in believing such nonsense about himself.

The minister was called in and had Robert kneel for the laying on of hands, a ritual calculated to drive out the demon. When the exorcism failed to work, Robert was told if he did not renounce his evil, they would be forced to excommunicate him from the church.

For a time Robert tried to conform. He attempted to deny his own inner urges, tried to accept the new life his family and church had laid out for him. He dated a young woman and even got engaged, but he finally realized that he was living out a lie. He knew he could never be married to a woman when his entire life was crying out to be in relationship with a man. Eventually Robert left home, and simultaneously he left the church of his childhood and youth, vowing he would never go to a church again. At nineteen he was homeless, churchless, and in the minds of most who had hovered over him as he grew up, he had also become godless. He left Texas for California and eventually made his way to Seattle.

Robert admits that during the years of his exile he did many things that were self-destructive and of which he is not proud. He felt betrayed by those who had once loved him and angry against God for making him the way he was. But gradually a new self began to emerge in Robert, a self that declared he was valuable just the way he was and that he had a right to be in this world. With it came a strong determination to show those who had excluded him that he could make it anyway. He was determined to become a productive citizen of society, regardless of society's lack of faith in him, that he would not allow himself to become embittered by rejection or denunciation, and that he would never turn his back on himself again by denying who he really was.

Robert did all he set out to do. Along with everything else, he became brave and tough. That little boy, who rode his bike to school and on his newspaper route and who obediently spouted scriptures as they were handed to him, grew up to become an activist for the cause of gay rights and a spokesman against bigotry and discrimination wherever he found it.

I met Robert in the early 1980s at an ecumenical prayer service for persons who were living with AIDS. It was the first time the Seattle churches had gotten together to say, "Look, we have a crisis on our hands. People are dying, many of them alienated by the church. We need to extend our ministry to include them and to let them know we care." I was invited to be the speaker at the service. Robert introduced himself when it was over, saying he had once been a Baptist and that he never expected to hear anything from a Baptist minister that he would even listen to. He said that perhaps he and his partner would visit our church service someday. I assured him they would be welcome, that we were an open church who welcomed all people from every walk of life.

I have often been asked what made me so open on the issue of homosexuality and why I speak out for it with such passion. It is simple. I despise bigotry or discrimination in any form. I feel the essence of Christ's teachings has to do with love and acceptance of all people. The only ones he ever castigated were the religionists of his day who "bound heavy burdens and laid them of the backs of others." He crossed every social barrier of his day to include all people in his great enterprise of the Kingdom of God. I do not feel I can do less and be a follower of his.

I also think that the soul in each of us is always in a process of evolution, and that some come here with many of the old battles of hatred and prejudice already fought and won. Maybe that is true of me. I know that I have instinctively felt the worth of all people since I was very young. I am as passionate about the rights of racial minorities as I am about sexual minorities. I always have been that way. It was never taught to me. It was just there inside of me from the first moment I ever started thinking about it. No one ever had to persuade me that we are all one. I have always known it as the monumental truth of our being.

I think it was G. K. Chesterton who said, "We have to love our neighbor simply because he is there. He is a sample of humanity given to us, and precisely because he may be anybody he is everybody." That resonates within me as a profound and enduring Truth. I am always puzzled when Christians cannot or will not see it.

I also need to say that the two churches I have pastored, one in Oakland and the other in Seattle, were both open and inclusive congregations. The Oakland church was 40 percent black, 10 percent Asian, 50 percent white when I left; the Seattle church is not as interracial, but it is strongly affirming of gays and lesbians. We adopted a Statement of Mission shortly after I came to the church in Seattle that expresses this philosophy:

> *We are a community of faith united in exploring what it means to follow the way of Jesus Christ, to be a people of God, and to love and care for our neighbors. As a church, we will know no circles of exclusion, no boundaries we will not cross, and no loyalties above those which we owe to God.*

Although I helped write the statement, it was the congregation who voted to accept it and to include it in our constitution. I do not stand alone in my conviction of the worth of all human beings. The people of the two churches I have served have lived it out as fully as I.

Thus when Robert and his partner, Dwight, came to visit our church, they found themselves warmly welcomed and invited to return. As Robert told me later, "No matter how tough you've become, it's always wonderful to be wanted." What I did not know when they came to our church was that Robert and Dwight were both HIV-positive. Dwight began to get sick about a year later and died rather suddenly. His family had always been caring and supportive of him. They grieved their loss while supporting Robert through his. Dwight's mother said to me, "I am so lucky to have been given a gay son. He has taught me so much."

A few years later Robert became sick. A reconciliation with his mother and sister was a touching event that I was privileged to share. His father had died some years earlier, refusing to the end to acknowledge that he had a gay son. Before his own death, Robert told me, "I love my family. I want you to say that at my funeral. I even love my dad. He did the best he could with me. Maybe someday the world will grow up and accept the things that can't be changed."

Death from complications arising from AIDS is not pretty. Dwight had suffered from dementia and was nearly blind at the end. Robert, on the other hand, seemed to have been spared the worst. He died quietly and without excessive pain. His last words to me were, "Thank you for giving me back the church and helping me find my faith again. I love you."

Robert had requested cremation and wanted his ashes scattered in the garden of the home he had owned with Dwight, near the place where Dwight's ashes had been strewn. His mother, his sister and one brother came for the funeral. Robert's oldest brother refused to come.

Why do we do to each other the sad and terrible things we do? Why have we not yet learned the simple theorem that true love is nondiscriminating. Why hasn't the church learned it? Again, I think it was Chesterton who said, "We make our friends; we make our enemies, but God makes our neighbor."

Acceptance is one of the primary joys in life. We all hunger for and need approval, appreciation and companionship of others. The basic loneliness that afflicts all humans will only be healed when we receive and extend acceptance.

When I see how difficult Robert's family and church made it for him, how he struggled and overcame in spite of their rejection, and how much joy he would have received from their acceptance, I am perplexed about why we inflict each other with such pain and loneliness. It puzzles and saddens me even more to see the Christian church doing the same thing, adding to the burdens that people already carry instead of seeking to lift them. What in God's name is the church if it is not a place of healing and acceptance, a place that offers primary joy to everyone?

Early in the advent of AIDS, a few fundamentalist preachers announced it was God's judgment being visited upon the homosexuals. Their small and twisted minds overlooked what health officials knew all along, that AIDS does not belong to any particular population. It belongs to all of us. Indeed, it began in Africa as a sexually transmitted disease among heterosexuals and in many countries is still predominant among heterosexuals.

Sometimes I wonder—as I remember Dwight's and Robert's deaths and the deaths of many other fine young people I have known—if maybe the homosexual community has not done something fine and wonderful for all of us. They were the first in this country to take on the disease. From them we learned most of what we know about this virus. From them we witnessed the heroic ways in which the young can meet death. Because of them and their friends, entire communities of people, straight as well as gay, were galvanized into arenas of compassionate service. Maybe the Age of AIDS is really the Age of Acceptance. Maybe that is the gift we will yet take from this terrible tragedy.

One of the things that Robert taught me is how critical it is that we accept ourselves if we are ever going to be able to accept others. We do not condition that acceptance on the basis of any forthcoming changes. We look deep inside ourselves to our true self, that part of us that is created in the image of God, and begin the work of remembering who we really are: a holy daughter or son of a living, loving God. At that level we not only celebrate our divinity, we also celebrate the common ground of our human sexuality. We are all sexual beings. Gay, lesbian, bisexual or straight, we have a common, shared capacity for warmth, affection and sexual intimacy. We all struggle with the same issues—trust, intimacy, isolation, commitment, fears of closeness with the same sex as well as the opposite sex. We have much more in common than we think. As we accept that common ground of sexuality, we will appreciate and honor the diversity of each.

After the death of his father, Robert wrote a letter to him. It was a kind of purging, a final good-bye that he was not allowed to say in this lifetime. He is not here to give his permission that it be reprinted, but somehow I think he would not mind. In its simplicity it is a word of grace to all of us on the spiritual discipline of Accepting.

Dear Dad,

There's seldom a day that goes by that I do not think of you. Now that you are gone, I think of you even more. I wish you had understood me better. Maybe then you would have accepted me. But then I am sure I did not understand you as well as I should. We just didn't have enough time in this life to ever reach that place of complete understanding, and that makes me sad. But I want to say that I love you anyway and I always will. You gave me life, and even if you didn't like what I am, I am still a part of you.

Since moving to Seattle I have learned something about the Eskimos, our neighbors to the north. When an Eskimo gets sick, he takes on a new name. I take it that maybe he believes he will get over the disease by leaving his old name and taking a new one. Sort of like fooling the sickness. If I thought taking on a new name would have rid me of the thing you once called my sickness and turned me into a son you could accept, I would have tried to do it. Except who I am is not a sickness. Nor is it a sin, as Reverend Gorbles said. It is the way God made me.

Maybe, Dad, if you could have loved and accepted me for who I am, I could have become even more. I guess I'll never know. I know I have a lot to learn yet. And I hope from wherever you are now that you're learning too and see it all differently. Maybe from up there you can then be a little proud of me again.

With all my love,
Your son Robert

There is much we could say on Acceptance, but what it comes down to is this: Wherever people are denied their fundamental rights of freedom and equity—as in the case of racial groups, women, homosexuals—the spiritual discipline of Acceptance needs to be applied. It is not a discipline to be practiced only on certain days or with certain people. It is our life work, as well as our passport to the next life, whatever and wherever that may be.

A Zen master once said that to seek one's true nature is a way to lead us to our long-lost home. To accept this life as it is, with all its wintry darkness, all its forked roads, all its awesome grandeur and amazing grace, and to accept those fellow travelers who come into our lives, some for brief moments and others for long years, is to accept the mysterious road that leads us back to God. The place that road begins is in the acceptance of our own true nature as a child of God. To that end, we journey with hope as our compass and love as our companion.

A Prayer of Accepting

Holy God, I will accept the truth about myself today. I will allow your light in me to shine upon this world. Remind me that your perfect love can cast out all fear. As I accept your love, allowing it to live in me, then the stranger becomes my brother or sister, the one I hated becomes my friend. And so I am freed to live in the harmony and oneness you have destined for all of us. Today I accept your will, for there is no other will for me to have. Your will alone can bring me happiness, so if I would have only what you can give, I must accept your will. In that will I shall remain as you created me. In your accepting love. Amen.

Spiritual Exercises for Accepting

1. Remember a time and situation where you found yourself feeling judgmental against someone. What caused your feelings of judgment: something the person said or did, the person's appearance, the person's representation of a cause you don't support or find offensive? Write about the incident in your journal. What was it that you found unacceptable about the person? What was your nonacceptance based on: parental teachings, strictures of a religious text, personal experience? What could that person have done to make himself or herself acceptable to you?

   Now examine how you responded. With avoidance? With disdain? By speaking your mind? By trying to convince the person of a better way? What does your response tell you about yourself?

   Finally, imagine a different response. Write a fictional scenario in your journal where you accept whatever it was you found unacceptable. Can you accept the person as worthy, even though you may not be able to accept what the person represents? While there are undoubtedly some things that are absolutely unacceptable in your moral framework, can you accept the person while not agreeing with what the person is? This is an exercise about yourself. What insights have come to you about the principle of acceptance as you have gone through this exercise?

2. Now turn the tables on yourself. Think about how you might be unacceptable to some person or group. What belief, habit or way of being do you have that others might find offensive? Write about these in your journal, asking the questions, Who would find me unacceptable and why? What can I do to make myself acceptable to them? Am I willing to do that? If not, why not? If it is impossible for you to change for the purpose of making yourself acceptable, why would you expect others to do that?

When you have completed the above exercises, meditate on this phrase: "That which I do not accept in others is that which I do not accept in myself." Do you believe this?

18

Realizing

*Blessed are those who realize they
have been created by love and for love,
for they shall live in love all the days of their lives.*

I sat out on the deck this morning and read the paper. It is late August, and there is a hint of autumn already in the air. There is paradox at the heart of autumn, a blend of transitoriness with confidence, a mixture of hope and despair. Autumn, perhaps more than any other season makes us aware that everything is more than it seems. I need that kind of assurance, particularly as I re-read the litany of woes and tragedies that stalked their way across the human landscape of a few years ago.

Hurricane Andrew has just blazed a thoroughfare through the southern parts of Florida and Louisiana, leaving a wake of damage that rates it as the most destructive natural disaster in American history. Rioting German youth who call themselves neo-Nazis are taking out their frustrations by attacking refugees from Romania and Vietnam. This violence, we are told, has its roots in the upheaval that followed the collapse of communism in East Germany, leaving millions jobless and youth who are willing to put their lives and the lives of others at stake because they regard life as basically worthless. Meanwhile, in pristine Idaho, my home state, the neo-Nazis of our own nation are in a standoff with U.S. federal forces. As if the wars within our own borders are not enough, the United States seems to be gearing up for another war in the Persian Gulf against Iraqi leader Saddam Hussein, a man that our country funded for years. Thousands are starving in Somalia, but Somali guerrillas loot the trucks carrying food and medical supplies to the refugees. And from Bosnia-Herzegovinia we are starting to hear reports of detention camps that parallel the Holocaust of the 1940s.

That is the report I recorded a few years ago. Every day there is a new list of horrors for us to read. We have almost become a world without edges when it comes to violence and inhumanity. What is wrong with us? Not satisfied with trashing our planet until we have seriously damaged its immune system, we are doing the same to the body of humanity. We are like a family that sets fire to their house and then, as they stand outside watching it burn, turn on each other.

I put down my journal and close my mind momentarily to what I have just read. I half close my eyes, squinting against the sun reflecting off the water, and everything seeps into everything else. The water and sky blur together, as in a Monet painting. And as I let my mind drift away from the reports I have just read and the anxieties that are eating away at the root of our existence, I remember something I read recently from a source I cannot recall: "The intimations which are but whispered, the

Presences which are but half-disclosed, are those which we should intently obey."

Father Thomas Keating, a Cistercian priest and modern-day contemplative, teaches what he calls the Centering Prayer. This is a discipline designed to withdraw our attention from the ordinary flow of thoughts to an awareness of the spiritual level of our being. I have used Keating's steps of discipline that he suggests in his book *Open Mind, Open Heart* and have found them to be helpful as a means of letting go of the outside world and taking hold of the inner. The goal here is not permanent escape from the world but temporary retreat, so that when we return, we bring a new realization of God's presence arising in the world's ordinary activities and daily events.[1]

Realization! That's it. There is more to this world—much more—than the litany of grief recited in the media. Beneath the surface of the polluted river of human activity there is a source that is quiet and pure. We can clear some of the debris floating on the surface of the river by resting our thoughts on the inner stream of consciousness, which is our participation in God's being. We can actually and literally purify our world of some of its debris by tapping into that pure river of consciousness that comes from God. It all has to do with our own powers of realization!

Realize. To convert from the imaginary or the fictitious into the actual or the real. To bring into concrete evidence. To impress upon the mind as truth. What a word! What a challenge!

The spiritual life tells us that we find by losing. We receive by giving. We live by dying. We know by not knowing. We become something new by ceasing to be something old. We learn to trust by risking. We become real by ceasing to be what we are not. So following this line of paradox, we may say that we learn to see the visible by first learning to see the invisible. The treasure is within.

It is like finding the Me below the me or below the three me's that H. A. Williams talks about. There is the me I put on for the benefit of others; there is the me I put on for my own benefit; and there is the me that I have locked out of sight because it is damaged and made ugly by the adversities of life. But beneath these three finite me's is another me—"the me in which there is something infinite, the me where God and fullness dwell."[2]

This is what I call my true self, my Christ self, the final me, and it is from that fullest self or final me that true realization comes.

We are created by love, to live in love, for the sake of love. That is the simple ground of our existence. It is a truth that springs from our fullest self, out of which arises both our human differences and our divine oneness, as well as our highest realizations.

But not until that truth is converted into concrete living does it mean anything to us other than a simple arrangement of words on paper. Truth that is not realized is only theory. Once realized, it changes into fact, a fact translated into reality by a new pattern of living, which then becomes a principle that mysteriously transforms the entire world.

One summer I was driving from Seattle to Arco, a distance of more than seven hundred miles. I was traveling alone, since Beverly had to remain in Seattle for an educators workshop. I was passing through Pendleton in eastern Oregon. It was so hot you could have fried an egg on the sidewalk. Under an overpass, I saw a man thumbing a ride. He had a pitiful look about him, wiping the perspiration from his forehead with an old red bandana and looking at me with a kind of urgency that seemed to say, "Please rescue me from this heat."

As I passed him, I thought how fortunate I was to have an air-conditioned car to take me where I was going. Then I heard within myself the voice that I have come to recognize as that which speaks from my higher self: "*Go back and get him.*"

I will *not*, I answered. I know better than to pick up hitch-hikers. But the orders kept hammering at my mind. I argued with it to the next exit, yet every argument I advanced was met with the firm directive: "*Go back and get him.*"

Well, I'll just swing back and see if he's still there, I reasoned, as I turned off the exit and made my way back down the freeway. Surely he will be gone by now. But he was still there. I crossed over the freeway to where he was standing. As I braked to a stop, I wondered what I was doing.

He came running toward the car, favoring one leg, but with the most eager look I have seen on a human face in a long time. "I'm a-thankin' ya'," he muttered, as he got in.

"I'm not going very far," I warned, as we started off, which was an outright lie. I had five hundred miles or more to go. He answered in a southern twang that was almost undecipherable, "A mile er two'll be mos' 'preciated."

He brought into the car an assortment of odors, none of them pleasant. He had the smell of not having bathed in days plus the drifting aroma of dank fields. Now see what you've got me into, I groused at the unseen messenger who had directed me into this venture and who was no doubt chuckling over the plight of my offended olfactories.

"Where are you going?" I asked, hoping he would say to the next turnoff. When he said, "West Virginia," my heart sank. "How do you happen to be so far from home?" I queried, not because I cared but because talking was better than sitting there silently drawing in his smell. I didn't have to ask if West Virginia was his home; his speech clearly betrayed it was.

So began his story. He had come to the Pacific Northwest to work on a construction job with a cousin. There was no work in West Virginia. He sent his check home each month to his wife and children, keeping only enough for his living expenses. The job ended, so he went to the bus depot in Seattle to buy a ticket home. Inside the depot he was abruptly jostled by three young men, who apologized and left hurriedly. Only when he got to the ticket counter did he realize they had taken his wallet. He had less than a dollar in change.

He sat down and philosophically worked out his next step. He wrote a card to his wife, telling her to look for him when he got there, and started hitchhiking. It had taken him two days to get from Seattle to Pendleton. No one seemed to want to pick him up. He had slept out the last two nights, grateful that it had not been cold.

As I listened, I became involved in his story. I instinctively knew he was telling the truth. When I asked him why he didn't phone his wife for money, he explained simply she had no phone; besides, the money he had been sending home was barely feeding the family. When I asked how he felt toward the men who had robbed him, he replied he didn't have to answer for what they did, and besides getting mad wasn't really going to hurt them, and it certainly wouldn't do him any good. His philosophy was simple: "They'se got t'anser fer themselves."

We had now crossed the Blue Mountains and were approaching LaGrande. He looked at the river and speculated that if he camped there, he could possibly catch some fish, if he had a pole. It occurred to me he was hungry. I asked when he had eaten last. As I suspected, he had eaten nothing since Seattle. I stopped in LaGrande and suggested we get a bite of lunch. He hesitated. "I'd be beholin' t'ya," he protested weakly. I assured him his company had made the trip easier for me and that it would be a pleasure to share lunch with him.

When we went into the restaurant, I was conscious for a brief moment of our disparities. The waiter who came to seat us looked at me, then at him, and back at me before asking snobbishly, "One for lunch?" It seemed a bit pretentious for LaGrande. I took certain pleasure in answering, "Two."

He went to the restroom to clean up and came back with his hair slicked down. There was a kind of painful dignity to him, despite his rustic appearance. He was reluctant to order from the menu. I wondered if he could even read it. Then I asked him if he liked steak. He said it was his favorite. I ordered him a steak dinner. He ate gratefully, telling me he would not soon forget my kindness.

Back in the car he asked me about myself. When I told him I was a minister and that I was going home to see my mother, who was aging and not very well, he said, "I knowed you wuz a man o' God. I jes' knowed you wuz."

"You're a man of God, too," I insisted, but he just shook his head. As we drove, I thought of the limits of his life. He had worked hard at menial jobs all his life, was probably barely literate, and would never be more than what he was at the moment. Yet he had a humble, honest spirit. He had asked me for nothing but was grateful for everything. He had always been poor, would always be poor, and would probably die with very little more than he had at this moment.

We in the more privileged positions of life sometimes wonder what we should do with the incompetents, the misfits, the disabled ones of this world, those who go through life four steps behind every opportunity and end up a drain and an embarrassment to the rest of us who have managed to make a modest success of our lives. I think now I know. We can only love them, hold them when we can, help them when it is possible, and pray for them, because their road is harder than ours and not destined to get easier. We can only try to lift them up, and failing that, remember that above all, they belong to us. And never, never should we fall into the trap of thinking ourselves superior to them. As Chesteron reminds us, precisely because they are anybody, they are everybody. Which meant that man at my side was also me.

Forgotten now was the smell. It was no longer there, or at least I was not aware of it. When I dropped him off just outside Boise, I gave him enough money for him to eat during the rest of his trip. I didn't do it to make me feel better. I did it because I knew I was supposed to. He tried to refuse it, even though he desperately needed it, but when I said it was what God wanted me to do, he took it with a kind of wonder. Then as he stood there beside the car, he bowed his head and said a prayer for me. "O Jesus, bless this good man. Keep 'im well an' strong, an' bless his mama who is sick and all his fambly. An' thank ya fer his kindness to me in my hour o' need. In yer own sweet and precious name. Amen."

I left him standing there at the edge of the highway and did not know until I was farther down the road that my eyes were wet with tears. His prayer, sweet and simple, and his own uncluttered goodness had touched my heart. I realized he possessed a kind of wealth that eluded many people who were better off materially than he. Most of all I realized he had been there for me and that if I had not obeyed the voice that told me to pick him up, I would have missed the blessing of oneness that came with our encounter.

Now don't go about picking up hitchhikers just because of this story. That is generally a foolhardy and dangerous thing to do in this day. But we should always travel with souls quiet enough to hear the holy word that is whispered to us and with wills ready to obey what we hear.

As I drove away from this man, I found myself asking aloud, "Now, what was all that about?" And I heard the words clearly spoken in my mind, "*That we might get your attention.*"

Suddenly I realized I was not alone. I had the distinct feeling that other entities were in the car with me. Then began one of the most amazing experiences of my life, so amazing, in fact, that I hesitate to write about it. For the next several hours I actually held conversation with these beings. I would ask a question aloud, and the answer would clearly unfold in my mind.

I was told that they were my teachers (some might call them guardian angels) from the other side who had been assigned to work with me. I was also told that it was time for me to stop relying so heavily on what other writers and thinkers have said and to listen to my own truth. I was told that my major assignment in this lifetime is to be a messenger, to give witness to a message of oneness and inclusion, even when ecclesiastical fingers wag at me reprovingly. I was also told that I would always have their assistance in that work and that I could continue vital and alert to the end of my days if I would follow that path and do certain necessary things to maintain my physical being.

There was more, but I choose not to share it all. I hesitate to talk about this kind of experience, for it has not been the norm for me, and too often it can be misunderstood or sought for the wrong reasons. I see it now as a rare moment in time when I was given a clear and unmistakable glimpse into the invisible world that surrounds all of us but that is not always perceived or trusted when it is glimpsed.

That day marked a perceptible shift for me in terms of sermon preparation and writing. The imperative changed from reading to listening. Preaching was no longer a task but a spiritual discipline. As I continued the process of trying to realize the value and importance of each moment, both on the seen and unseen levels, the doors of insight seemed to swing open more totally for me than they ever had before.

Shortly after that came my wilderness dream, and out of that dream came this book. That mysterious man on the road was the catalyst for a sudden shift within me that first sent me back across my early years and then directed me to look forward to what is yet to come. He evoked for me the natural religion of my early childhood, when heaven and earth were one and God was the companion who rode my horse with me over the prairies and hills. But soon my child's eyes were clouded over by ideas and opinions, preconceptions and abstractions. Not until years later did I become aware that a vital sense of mystery had been lost and that there was a hollow place in me filled with longing.

We become seekers without knowing what we seek. We would be foolish to want to return to our childhood, for that is not a truly enlightened place. I suppose at the very least we all want a sense of well-being, times when the clutter of ideas and emotions can fall away and the body and mind can merge into unity with the spirit, returning to their natural harmony with all creation.

But it is not easy. For one thing, there is a core of suffering that seems to afflict all creation. A woman once asked me if spiritual formation must always arise out of suffering and the dark night of the soul. It seemed to her that those who manifested a bent for the contemplative life were often those who had suffered. She wanted to know if spirituality could not also rise out of happiness, whether it is possible to become free from emotional pain, or perhaps avoid it altogether.

I doubt that it is possible to avoid suffering altogether. Certainly some individuals have more of it than others, but it is still the common denominator of human existence. Even if one could transcend personal pain and suffering by evolving to a kind of ecstatic state of spiritual consciousness, one should never be able to reach a point where the pain of others is of no consequence. In a world crying out in desperate need for healing and release, a spiritually evolved person could no more escape an empathic suffering with those caught in prisons of despair than clear water could avoid becoming muddy when it storms. Pain and joy go together.

However, once suffering is accepted completely, it ceases in a way to be suffering. It becomes a friend with whom we live, who gives to our faith the enrichment necessary for growth, and who helps us discover the joy that emerges from pain. We can never fully explain suffering, try though we might, and we should never forget that for many it is a daily reality. But life should not be overruled by suffering. Even in this wilderness of world suffering, there can still be periods of great happiness, compensations of sunlit moments, when the world is seen as a beautiful place filled with the goodness of God.

There is a highway carved through the heart of the Rocky Mountains that slips continually in and out of little black tunnels, bored through the stone canyon walls. As one travels that highway, the route is alternated between splashes of golden sunlight shining on sweeping vistas of sky and domed mountains and black blotches where nothing is visible except tiny pinpoints of light at the end of the tunnel.

It occurs to me that life is very much like that highway. The challenge is to carry the light into the darkness and to focus on the blackened areas as intently as we revel in the sunny spaces. We cannot always control the rhythms of life, any more than we can control the weather. But if we have a grounding in the solitary center of our being, in the final Me, we will not be dependent on any outer circumstance or situation to maintain. Nor will we allow our moods and wilfulness to get in the way of what we must be and do.

I suppose to some extent spirituality does rise out of suffering, essentially because we cannot avoid suffering at some level. It is as much a part of life as joy. By that I don't mean to imply that everyone has had a wretched childhood, as some psychotherapists would have us believe. My wife Beverly had a classically happy childhood. Mine was more difficult, but I would not change any of it if I could. All of it has been meaningful. We take whatever we have had into the spiritual life, for that is all we have.

Miserable people are no better candidates for the spiritual life than contented people. Besides, misery and contentment are not things that have been done to us. They are what we choose. We can be miserable as long as we want to, or we can determine to realize a joy even in the midst of trying circumstances. Our childhood is over, and locating the hurt child in our psyche has to stop sometime so that we can begin to attend to the adult part of ourselves that is infinitely wiser and more capable than the child could ever hope to be.

We cannot avoid suffering. It is as much a part of life as joy. But suffering has in it the seeds of decay and temporality; joy is pervasive and eternal. Spirituality is based to a certain degree on a tension between the two, which is essentially a tension between what one is now and what one hopes to be tomorrow. The ground out of which this tension springs is alive and gracious, bringing forth abundantly. Therefore, we are always called to live in openness, wonder and gratitude, as we realize our own wonderful and mysterious life. In that life is stored everything we need: the possibility of forgiving everything, of treasuring everything, and of knowing everything that we need to know.

I read recently that some psychologists have now decided that people who live in climates that are predominantly overcast and marked by shorter days tend to become easily depressed and discouraged. So something called "light therapy" has been developed. You sit in front of fluorescent panels for a few hours each day. This apparently has the effect of lengthening the day as far as the body is concerned, so the body is fooled into believing spring or summer is here. The results show that depressed people get better without drugs or therapy, just by being exposed each day to light.

I have no way to evaluate the merit or need of light therapy for anyone else. I do know that living in the Pacific Northwest, where winters are generally characterized by long periods of overcast weather, has not affected me adversely. Indeed, I tend to be more productive in such a climate, more content to work at cerebral tasks. Prolonged periods of sunshine often beguile me either into a kind of sluggish inactivity or a frantic scurrying about to enjoy the sunshine while it is here. For me, a climate of any kind of continuous weather pattern, sunny or otherwise, would become monotonous. I thrive best on the changing rhythms of the seasons.

We are each different in this respect. But no matter how we respond to weather, there is a place of sacred realization inside all of us, where we can tune in to a fuller level of reality that is always present and in which we are invited to participate. I am not suggesting any particular method by which you might do this. I am more and more convinced that each person has his or her own path to follow to that center of realization. Yoga does it for some, jogging does it for others. For a period in my life I used a disciplined pattern of meditation that was a composite of several systems I had studied. It doesn't matter what path you choose as long as your fundamental desire is to open to God. The important thing, as Father Keating reminds us, is to keep your attention on the source of the river rather than what is passing along its surface. And remember it is a lifetime work. There is no such thing as instant enlightenment or complete realization. If your intention is pure, the process will always be beneficial and the result will always be one of realization.

Spiritual realization does not always guarantee spiritual conformity. The mystics will know each other by the language that is spoken because they have traveled to the same country. Likewise, the fundamentalists will use certain phrases and expressions that are characteristic of that particular religious experience. A friend once observed that the mystic is mystical and the fundamentalist is fundamental, and never the twain shall meet. But I am not inclined to agree. I was practically a fundamentalist in the fervor of my early Christian years, because that was the environment in which I was nurtured. I have known a number of people who have moved from fundamentalism to a more open expression of spirituality, although they might disavow that fundamentalism had ever really taken hold of them, even when they were espousing it. But I think we all change when we want to.

I do not accept the fundamentalist point of view today, but I do accept the fundamentalist. It is my acceptance of the fundamentalist *as a fundamentalist* that is the basis for my evaluations. I know some fundamentalists who are loving, accepting people, some who love me even though they do not agree with me at most levels. I hold out to them their right to believe as they wish and only ask that they do that for me. That is precisely what many of them will not do. Their fundamentalism insists that they be intolerant, judgmental and nonaccepting of anything that does not conform to their own point of view. Although they have a right to their beliefs, no one has a right to be bigoted and prejudicial. I think that is contrary to God's will.

What are the similarities and differences between the fundamentalist and the mystic? The only similarity would be their common passion for Christ-likeness and Christ-centeredness. Their differences are many. The fundamentalist claims to be a literalist when it comes to the Bible, accepting every word, just as it is written, as divinely inspired—hence, their name. The mystic would be more inclined to regard the scriptures as a human record of God's activity in human history, a record that tried to be faithful but unavoidably made mistakes and misinterpretations. The fundamentalist becomes evangelistic, spiritually extroverted, eager for conversions, and dedicated to the Great Commission of Christ, that is, "Go into all the world and preach the gospel." The mystic becomes reflective, inward-looking, soul-searching, contemplative. The mystic regards the spiritual life as a journey, whereas the fundamentalist would see it as an event, namely, salvation accomplished through Jesus Christ. The mystic would allow for differing interpretations of Jesus and the Bible, while the fundamentalist would insist on only one. The mystic believes it is his duty to plant and nourish spiritual values; the fundamentalist believes it is his mission to harvest them. And so it goes.

As far as we can tell, Jesus was at odds with the fundamentalism of his time. His criticisms of the Pharisees (and these were harsh and severe criticisms) did not mean that he did not accept them. He accepted them at the exact levels where they presented themselves, saw them for what they were, and encouraged them to be more than they thought they could be.

Acceptance must always be tempered by realization. Certain things ought not to be accepted. Both mystic and fundamentalist would agree to that. But the fundamentalist would use an external standard, the Bible, for that determination, and the mystic would rely on the inner voice of Spirit. Having said all that, I want to say that labels are misleading, often inaccurate and generally unfair. They have the capacity to polarize rather than bring together. Underneath the surface of all our external loyalties there is a common yearning for God. If we can remember that about one another, perhaps we will be gentler and more supportive of one another, no matter what we call ourselves or what path we choose to follow.

I was trying to get on the Seattle freeway one evening during rush hour, but it was a difficult job. The on-ramp was jammed, and traffic was barely moving. The faces of people in their cars reflected a variety of emotions: annoyance, impatience, eagerness. Some honked their horns and made obscene gestures if someone cut in front of them. Others played their radios and tried to relax. Suddenly it occurred to me we were all doing the very same thing. We were trying to get home. Every person in that tie-up wanted to be home and was trying to get there as quickly as possible. With that realization I was filled with a profound love for everyone and an overwhelming sense of our common destination.

It is true for all of us. More than anything else, we want to go Home. And it is on the wings of love we get there.

A Prayer of Realizing

You have blessed me constantly on my way, and I have not always realized it. I hear the news reports of disasters and misdeeds and wonder where you are. Help me to pierce the veil that hides the truth and to see your hand at work in every event and every person that is on this earth. Help me to discern between the real and the false, between that which is eternal as against that which is temporal and illusory. Help me to touch the eternal truth within myself, the love that comes from you, and which will help me live from my highest and best. May I go forth in faith, knowing that I do not walk alone and that I will never lose the way again, for what is here begun will grow in life and strength and hope forever. In your love I pray. Amen.

Spiritual Exercises
for
Realizing

Realizing is not a spiritual principle that is achieved quickly. It is a discipline that goes on and on as the whole self comes together and moves forward with life. It begins like the first feathery tips of green pushing through the softening ground, telling you that a flower is on its way. Then one day, like a crocus in spring, it suddenly blossoms without your being aware of it. The following exercises can help you plant the seed of realizing.

1. *Cultivation of the soil.* Over the course of a week, stop at least three times during the course of a day and look around you. Don't analyze, just observe. Observe people, their behavior, their expressions. Observe how light casts itself through a window and over the earth. Sense how a chair feels beneath your body, how the ground feels beneath your feet. As you observe the soil in which your life is planted, try to sense the Spirit that is behind the physical manifestation of people and objects, the Eternal Reality that is behind the movement of time. Try to realize your world by seeing through new eyes. Quiet your mind from its usual flurry of meaning-making and just observe. Write in your journal what you see.

2. *Planting the seed.* During this week of soulful observing, each night reflect on whether you have had any glimpse of the numinous—of the God-filled moment. As you close your eyes before falling asleep, still your mind to receive the revelation and any learning that your observation may have brought. What you are doing is practicing God-realization, making room for moments in your life when you can feel consciously connected to the Divine Life that lives itself through you.

3. *Observing the flower.* After a week of quiet observing, start a new week of self-observation. Watch yourself interact with others, doing a mundane chore, hugging a child, climbing the stairs, brushing your teeth. Consider your action as part of a great luminous web of Being. Realize yourself as part of that web, connected to the Whole. Write in your journal about any time when you experienced a moment of God-realization, a moment when you felt totally in the embrace of that which is the source of your life.

19

Rejoicing

Blessed are those who rejoice at all times and in all circumstances, knowing that God is in everything with eternal joy. Through them the seed of love will be eternally resown and they shall stand tiptoe in the bright kingdom of the moment, awakening the universe with their astonishing smile.

I once heard E. Stanley Jones, the great Methodist missionary, say, "If you're a Christian, you ought to notify your face." He meant that the essential and underlying ingredient of the spiritual life is joy and that joy ought to be reflected in how we act, look and feel. Life can be lived at various extremes, between freedom and dependence, faith and doubt, love and hate, action and passivity, self-possession and self-giving. These are normal tensions. But always there should be a pervasive and imbricating sense of joy forming the synthesis between the two poles.

The spiritual way is not through a labyrinth of old stone paths hollowed by many steps, such as one finds when following the way of the cross through the streets of old

Jerusalem. The spiritual way is through the unexplored regions and unattended depths of our own well-being, through the new wilderness of our particular age, until we come to the place of complete and total trust. Questions may not all be answered to our satisfaction, and truth may remain elusive, but we will know that we have been found by God, a God we can trust absolutely and forever. With that knowing, joy will come to dwell in us, and we shall know what it is to savor each moment for its own revelation of truth and to adore all creation for its constant shower of grace.

Because Jesus taught that God had poured Godself into humankind, it is inevitable that in God's kingdom humankind must become one. Hence, the responses of those who would celebrate the kingdom is to show mercy and justice toward one's neighbors. God has disappeared into humankind, and to serve and honor God means to serve and honor each other. The joy cannot be hoarded. It has to be shared, for it belongs to all. True joy is contagious and infectious. If it is the real thing, it spills out to others. And thus the human race advances a step higher in its spiritual evolutionary process, just because a single believer agrees to share the joy.

We have talked about the suffering that plagues the footsteps of humankind. But there is a joy in this universe that has a power all its own, a joy that is both independent of us and yet a part of the inner climate of each. It is a gift available to us by sitting still occasionally and being willing to receive it, by awakening within ourselves to that which is already there waiting to be discovered.

Jesus gave us this joy when he offered us the wondrous possibility of God-with-us. He said the kingdom is in our midst now. We are not waiting for our future. We are living our future at this moment. What is required is that we let go of life in order to receive it. We are invited to forget ourselves on purpose, so that we might catch a glimpse of God. When that happens, no matter how fleeting or transitory the glimpse, we begin to rejoice, for we know that we are loved, and we know that we are safe.

Kabir, the fifteenth-century Indian poet, was a Moslem whose spiritual growth was influenced by Sufis and Hindus. Among his many poetic lines are these three, which I have followed with brief personal comments:

1. "The fish in the sea is not thirsty."[1]

   The fish has everything it needs. So do we. Everything is in harmony as it should be.

2. "The only woman awake is the woman who has heard the flute."[2]

   Something always calls us out of our sleep to the deeper truth of life, if we are willing to listen. The wake-up call has been sounded for those who have ears to listen.

3. "The Guest I love is inside me!"[3]

   We can search for a God outside ourselves whom we can influence and thus love, but only as we touch the divine within ourselves can we love the God of history, the God of the universe, and the God that indwells all creation.

The Gnostics taught that we learn to love only by learning to hate. If we do not first struggle against, we will not be drawn toward, be it ourselves or another. Love exists within us but is only released when we learn to love. This love is neither a doctrine nor an international agreement. It is what lives within us as a possibility. It abides eternally, for it is the very movement and activity of the soul itself. Our spiritual lives can reach the point where the soul simply begins to radiate love rather than merely performing altruistic deeds of kindness.

If we would discover the absolute of love, we have to cut all ties and regard everything, every face and every blade of grass, without reference to any other thing, as though it were the only thing that existed in the world. We have to delete our constant impulse to judge and our ready instinct to make comparisons. We simply accept whatever is before us and immerse ourselves in it totally. We give it a moment of rapt attention, an attention that is really rooted in eternity. In this way we find the love that nourishes and connects all things, the love that is the foundation for joy and the taproot of life.

Jacob Needleman, Jewish professor and author, believes that the essential expression of Christian love is helping one's neighbor, but he does not equate this with some sort of noble response to the suffering need of another person. Rather, he sees love fulfilled when we are willing to transmit the truth to another by nurturing the growth of his or her soul. That means that loving one's neighbor is to assist the arising and unfolding of the neighbor's soul. Needleman says that emotional Christianity is morally blind and intellectual Christianity is morally powerless. But to love another in such a way that the soul can be loved is Christianity at its highest. True love, then, is soul love, love that comes from one soul and nourishes or awakens the soul of another.[4]

I had a dream not long ago that was vivid and puzzling. In the dream I was at a retreat. It was early morning, and I wakened to the sound of happy voices outside my window. I looked out and saw people from my church, drinking coffee and chatting happily in the gray dawn. They were people I knew and loved. Then I saw a man and woman coming down an embankment in our direction, but the woman stumbled, fell, and then rolled down the hill, stopping next to my window and in front of the other people who were standing nearby. Her male companion ran down to help her. And what did I do? I pulled the covers up over my head and went back to sleep. Except I didn't. I awoke disquieted and guilty. At first I interpreted the dream as a personal indictment of my refusal to help another. I could justify my action by saying that there were others who could help.

I puzzled over the dream for several days as I reviewed what I knew about dream interpretation. Dreams are primarily about the one who dreams them, not someone else, and this one had me puzzled and concerned.

Then one day it came to me. The fall down the hill represented a spiritual fall, symbolizing obstacles in the path. The woman, representing my spiritual self, was urging me to overcome the obstacle in my path, an obstacle that had to do with love. The man hurrying down to help the woman was also me, my altruistic self. But love is more than lifting up a fallen one and more than emotional reaction to the suffering of another. My turning over in bed and covering my head, looking away from the traditional approach of solving the problem, was an indication that I am now obliged to doubt the value of caring actions that emerge only from emotion or moralism. Reactions and commitments that spring forth when we have perceived the pain of another are often just aspects of egoism. "I am helping this person up, because this is what I am expected to do by those who are watching."

The dream instructed me to turn my back on that approach and to concentrate on the unfolding of that in me which can harmonize the real elements of my nature. I am all the persons in my dream. As I accept and care for the various elements of my own nature, I assist in the arising of a new principle of energy and love in myself. The strengthening of this new energy of love in my own nature will be for the blessing of all and not just for me alone. I may not know quite all that is involved in loving in such a manner that I nurture the growth of the soul in others, but I am learning. My own soul is teaching me.

Carl Jung once said instead of waging war on ourselves, it is better for us to learn to tolerate ourselves and to convert inner difficulties into real experiences. We are all too prone, I think, to transfer to others the injustice and violence we have received from others or that we inflict upon ourselves. Love is indeed the Guest who lives inside each of us as the taproot of our lives, and it always calls us to a better way, the way of rejoicing and thanksgiving.

Although I went kicking and screaming into the ministry, I have had some of my greatest joy in being a pastor. The opportunity to share in people's lives at deep and meaningful levels, the challenge of framing sermons that represent my own searching and can touch the searching hearts of the people who are willing to listen to me, to be the recipient of such a tender outpouring of love from many, to be challenged to grow spiritually, not just as a luxury but as a necessity in order to sustain and maintain one's own being—these have been some of the reasons that I literally rejoice when I think of the ways ministry has blessed my life. For those who know themselves called to it, ministry is truly a sacred life.

But like any other profession, it has its pitfalls and delusions, its inordinate demands and confusions. The joy of ministry, where pastor and people make a commitment to one another, is not unlike a marriage of two people. We want a marriage to bring us contentment, and we make our commitment in that hope. But commitment and contentment do not always go hand in hand. Our best intentions sometimes get thwarted or delayed.

I had a wedding once that contained more blunders and pitfalls than should have to be endured. To begin with, the bride's mother somehow thought the wedding was hers. Karen, the bride, had almost nothing to say about any of it. Her mother chose the date, the dress, the place of the reception, along with the details and particulars that went with it. She had not chosen Neal, the groom, and that may have occasioned her with some resentment. But she managed to overcome it and to alleviate her annoyances by plunging into the preparations feverishly and totally. By the time we arrived at the actual wedding, Karen was so nervous and distraught from Mother's pulling and controlling, she was practically insensate. "I'm afraid I'll forget what to do," she confessed to me, as we waited for the processional to begin.

"Just listen to me, Karen," I answered. "I will be telling you what to do. You don't have to remember a thing except to do what I tell you."

Just then a bald, rumpled-looking fellow staggered into the foyer and lurched his way down the aisle. The organist had already started the wedding march, and here was some drunk stumbling forward. "Wait a minute," I whispered to the wedding party. I marched down the aisle behind the fellow, took him by the arm, and said quietly, "Follow me, please." His breath nearly knocked me over right there in the aisle, but he came along obediently. I led him to the front of the church, took him over to the right, opened a door that led outside into an alley, pushed him through it, and made my way back to the foyer. A slight gasp and titter went through the congregation, but I felt somewhat pleased that I had dispensed with a potential problem with such ease.

The procession of the wedding party began. The groom, minister and groomsmen marched down the side aisle and fanned out in front. The bridesmaids began their stately procession down the center aisle. I noticed Karen's mother glaring at me, as though I had done something wrong, but I put it out of my mind. Now Karen was entering on the arm of her father. She was halfway down the aisle, when to my horror I saw the same old fellow I had just escorted into the alley staggering down the aisle behind her. He had obviously made his way along the outside of the church, found the front door, and had reentered. He was determined somehow to go to this wedding.

What to do? Karen and her father had now arrived at the front of the church, Neal had stepped into place beside them, but where was the drunk? He had reeled into the seat next to Karen's mother, where he was sitting down, wiping his brow with a grimy handkerchief. Karen's mother was looking straight ahead, as though she were not even aware of him. I couldn't help but admire her composure. She was not going to allow this bum the opportunity of spoiling this moment for her. This wedding was hers, by golly, and she would enjoy it to the hilt or know the reason why.

The drunk fellow sat there quietly, trying to hold his head erect but unable to focus his eyes anywhere. When Karen's father went back to be seated next to his wife, after having given the bride away, there was no place for him to sit. To my utter amazement he sat down anyway, practically on top of the intruder, who was now squeezed in tightly between Karen's parents. I could not believe how beautifully they were all handling all of it.

By now Karen and Neal had reached the kneeling altar in front of me where the rest of the ceremony would take place. I usually make it a custom to speak a personal word about the meaning of marriage to a couple as part of the ceremony. I glanced at Karen. She looked vague, as though she was not sure where she was at the moment. I began to speak by addressing both of them by name, "Karen, Neal."

As I paused, to my utter consternation, Karen knelt. She had remembered my instructions to do exactly as I said, and mistaking her groom's name for the command "Kneel," she did just that. I looked at Neal and his facial expression registered confusion. I did the only thing I could think of. I said, "Karen, rise." She stood up obediently, and the ceremony went on. I was not even sure she knew what she had done. She was behaving like a wind-up doll.

Midway through the vows, the best man began to hiccup. These were not gentle little hics. They reverberated through the sanctuary like gunshots. I might have expected it from the drunk in the front row but not from the best man. He stood ramrod straight, his face flushed and his hands clenched. The hiccups increased in volume. As he tried desperately to restrain them, they became more explosive and almost convulsive. Indeed, they became so forceful he couldn't get the ring off the pillow when it came time. Each time he tried to untie the ribbon holding it, he would erupt into a gut-wrenching "HIC!" His fingers were shaking to the point he could not control them. At last, in desperation, he grabbed the pillow from the little boy who was designated ring-bearer and thrust it at me.

This ring-bearer had been well coached. He was five years old and knew what was supposed to happen. Thus he knew giving up the pillow was not in the script. As he felt it wrested from his hands, he piped in a treble voice that everyone could hear, "Hey, just the ring, not the piller!"

By now I had extended the pillow to Neal, asked him to remove the ring, and I was able to hand the pillow back to the little lad before he started a riot. He took it and with grim vengeance swung it against the rear end of the best man as a reprimand. It was the right thing to do. The hiccups came to a sudden and much-welcomed end.

There was a moment at the very end, after I pronounced Karen and Neal husband and wife, when everything seemed to come together. They looked at each other with such love in their eyes, such tenderness and devotion, that a holy hush seemed to come over the whole congregation. Karen had finally arrived at her own wedding. She knew where she was and what she was doing. Her mother may have claimed everything prior, but that moment was hers, theirs. I didn't have to invite them to embrace. They moved into each other's arms and kissed as fervently as two people possibly could in front of several hundred guests. They'll make it, I thought to myself. She will never remember anything that went wrong, she'll only remember this wonderful moment at the end. As for Neal, he loves her enough to endure her mother's interference and even to go through a formal wedding against his own wishes. They'll be there for each other from now on. I was as sure of it as I ever have been with a couple.

There was one more uncomfortable moment. At the reception I went to the bride's mother to apologize for the drunken intruder who had wormed his way into the seat beside her. She replied icily, "Dr. Romney, that was my brother. He was unavoidably detained and couldn't make it on time."

Her brother? Karen's uncle? I had unceremoniously ushered him into the alley. Unavoidably detained? One need not speculate long to know where. But Karen and Neal were now married. The future belonged to them. And among the hundreds of marriages I have performed through the years, theirs is one that stands out as truly unforgettable and strongly metaphorical.

Life in the parish has sometimes been for me like that wedding. There were times when nothing went right, when someone had a selfish grasp on things and wouldn't turn loose, when all our best plans seemed to be sabotaged by some demonic force.

But breaking through have been those delicious times when we knew that we were one in God's love, that we were part of an enterprise bigger than ourselves, and that we would make it through somehow. That's the kind of hope the human race wants.

We all want dead certainties as we move through life, but all we are offered are living possibilities. Those possibilities will offer us the chance to deal with funny uncles, domineering mothers, hiccups at inconvenient times, the dissolution of our fondest dreams, the death of our dearest love. Those are the pieces of which real life is made. And we get the chance to deal with all of it in the curious but supreme task of growing these souls of ours into maturity. When we can act out of an inner unity, then despite our mistakes and even because of them, we find the path of freedom leading through the wilderness.

Underneath every event and experience of life there is an element of joy, if we look long enough to find it. Nothing is ever wasted. Everything has meaning, and everything will lead us to God, the source of all joy, if we give attention to our lives. God comes to us clad in many forms—the careless terrors of nature, the repulsive masks of ruthlessness, the nameless dread of loneliness, and, yes, even in our own mistakes and misdeeds. God is there in all of it, for ultimately God is all there is. But since God is everywhere, in our suffering losses as in our victories, there is joy in everything, for wherever God is, love is. And where there is love, there is always joy.

There is no real end to this book. I will be writing it as long as I live, refining the old disciplines, finding new markers and expressing new truths as they are slowly assimilated into my life. I lay no claim to originality nor infallibility. Every concept I have learned and expressed has already been learned and expressed by someone else, perhaps in even better ways. They don't belong to any of us singly. They belong to all. My uniqueness is the same as yours—the individual experience. No one has ever lived life the same way I have, the same way you have, for we cannot be duplicated. No one else has to face the same exact wilderness that you or I face. Your wilderness is your own. It belongs to you and no one else. But we still need each other, for the wilderness of one is the wilderness of all.

In Chinese folklore, I am told, there is a mythical bird, who is only half a bird. It has one eye, one wing, one leg. In order to fly, a right-hand bird must find a left-hand bird. Alone they are earthbound, or we might say wilderness bound. But together they can soar into the sky.

We need each other if we are to be complete. We need each other if we are going to see our wilderness as the Garden of Eden, from which we each have come. We need each other as much as we need ourselves, for it is in the sacred depths of ourselves and one another that we find God, the All and the Only of our being.

Evening has come. Rain has drenched my promontory on the bluff for the last several days, but a wan sun peeks through the mists and makes a final caress of light. Beverly sits beside me, as she has now for nearly forty years, my companion and helpmate on this wilderness trek. And in my heart are the hundreds of others that have moved in and out of my life, each a part of God's Plan. As the light fades, I am remembering, I am treasuring, I am accepting, I am realizing. Yes, all of it. But most of all, I am rejoicing in the good darkness and the gentle light that will continue to direct me through the new wilderness of tomorrow.

A Prayer of Rejoicing

I rejoice that you hold my future, just as you hold my past and present. In your hands I rest serene and untroubled, sure that only good can come to me. The world is not my enemy, for I have chosen to be its friend. Everything I want is in you. You are the aim of all my living, the end I seek, my purpose and my function and my life. In you I am united with all living things. I thank you that your light shines forever in all of us. I walk with you in peace and holiness, rejoicing in the faith that what you have created in love you will also redeem in love. I go now to meet the newborn world, knowing that Christ has been reborn in it and that the holiness of this rebirth will last forever. In the name of your Son, Jesus the Christ, I pray. Amen.

Spiritual Exercises
for
Rejoicing

Rejoicing springs from gratitude. When we are truly grateful, our responses are naturally filled with joy, and joy expressed physically can be especially powerful. Some of the following exercises may help you express that joy.

1. *Body prayer.* Most of our emotions are held in our bodies. You can express joy by "praying with your body." One way to do this is to stand with both feet planted firmly, feeling yourself well grounded. Then stretch your arms upward, feeling your entire body reaching to touch the sky. Now swing your arms around in wide circles and begin to allow your body to turn with the movement. Slowly turn until you are facing 90 degrees to one side. As you face in the new direction, bring your hands together in an attitude of prayer and thanksgiving, and bow your head in gratitude to all the forces that guide and sustain life. Move this way through the four directions, offering a prayer to each direction. As you move, rejoice in the strength of your body and your good health, the sky above you and the earth beneath your feet. Let your movements be a spontaneous body prayer of gratitude and joy.

2. *Song and music.* Native North Americans and many other indigenous peoples have beautiful traditions of singing to commemorate events and life passages. Music is a powerful force for opening the soul. You might learn some hymns to sing, such as "Joyful, joyful, I adore you, God of glory, God of love." Or make up your own chant spontaneously. Music can also be a wonderful accompaniment to meditation. Find recordings that both soothe and elate your spirit, and play them as you sit quietly. If the music invites you to dance, move in response to the stirrings that it creates.

3. *Shift your perception.* Review the twelve wilderness markers, memorize the beatitudes for each marker, and chant one a day as a mantra. Whenever you feel down, look away from your problems and refocus your attention on God, who looked upon all that had been created, rejoiced over it, and said, "It is good." Repeat these words to yourself, letting them drift deep into your consciousness and heart. "It is good." "It is good." "It is good." So it was, is now, and shall be evermore. Peace and joy be yours. Amen.

God of the Wilderness

SLANE 10.10.9.10
Traditional Irish Melody
Harm. by David Evans, 1874–1948

Rodney R. Romney

1. God of the wilderness, God of the plain,
2. God of the elephant, God of the snail,
3. God of our planet, betrayed and misused,
4. God of all people whose love makes us one,
5. God of the wilderness, Eden's delight,

God of the torrent and soft summer rain,
God of the spider and God of the whale,
God of the people exploited, abused,
Help us to treasure the work You've begun.
Brooding o'er all with creative insight,

Father of darkness and Mother of light,
Father of vastness and Mother of small,
Your Birthing Spirit now sounds a command,
Help us to be who we came here to be,
Lure us to heights where your harmony rings,

Your Birthing Spirit will lead us aright.
Your Birthing Spirit wants union with all.
Urging a justice and peace for the land.
Serving and loving till all life is free.
Bringing connection with all living things.

Notes

Chapter 4

1. Rodney Romney, *Journey to Inner Space* (Nashville: Abingdon, 1980), p. 47.
2. Brother Lawrence, *The Practice of the Presence of God, 1692* (Philadelphia: Judson Press edition, 1942), p. 53.
3. Paul Tillich, *Systematic Theology*, Vol. 1 (Chicago: University of Chicago Press, 1951), p. 13.

Chapter 5

1. This poem is also attributed as a Chinese or Greek saying. The form quoted here is attributed to James Terry White in his book *Not by Bread Alone* (1907).
2. Thomas Moore, *The Care of the Soul*. (New York: Harper Collins, 1992), p. xviii.

Chapter 6

1. Eknath Easwaran, translator and Gita scholar, quoted by Wayne W. Dyer, *Real Magic* (New York: Harper Collins, 1992), p. 195.

Chapter 8

1. Riane Eisler, *The Chalice and the Blade* (New York: Harper Collins, 1987), pp. 80–103.

Chapter 9

1. Uri Shulevitz, *The Treasure* (New York: Farrar, Straus, Giroux, 1978).
2. *The Book of Angelus*, Silesius trans. by Frederick Franck.

Chapter 10

1. Annie Dillard, *Holy the Firm* (New York: Harper & Row, 1984), p. 50.

Chapter 12

1. Lewis Thomas, *A Long Line of Cells* (Camp Hill, PA: Book of the Month Club, 1990). This volume includes the major works of Thomas, including, *The Lives of a Cell.*

2. Viktor Frankl, *Man's Search for Meaning* (Boston: Beacon Press, 1962), p. 172.

Chapter 13

1. Geoffrey Wainwright, *Doxology, The Praise of God in Worship, Doctrine and Life* (New York: Oxford University Press, 1980), pp. 43–44.

2. *The Cloud of Unknowing,* translated into Modern English by Clifton Wolters (Harmondsworth, Middlesex, England: Penguin Books, 1961), p.61.

3. Howard Thurman, *The Inward Journey* (New York: Harper and Brothers, 1961), p. 50.

4. May Sarton, *Plant Dreaming Deep* (New York: Norton, 1968), p. 87-88.

Chapter 14

1. Clara Endicott Sears, *The Power Within* (privately published in 1911), p. 24.

Chapter 15

1. John Cheever, *The Stories of John Cheever* (New York: Alfred Knopf, 1978) pp. 128–136.

2. Henri Nouwen, *Compassion* (Garden City, New York: Doubleday and Company, 1982), p. 4.

3. Thomas Merton, *Contemplation in a World of Action* (Garden City, New York: Doubleday Image Books, 171) pp. 154–155.

4. Starr Daily, *You Can Find God* (Westwood, New Jersey: Fleming H. Revell, 1958), pp. 83–84.

Chapter 16

1. Lewis Smedes, *Forgive and Forget* (San Francisco: Harper & Row, 1984) pp. 3–38.

Chapter 18

1. Thomas Keating, *Open Mind, Open Heart, the Contemplative Dimension of the Gospel* (New York: Amity House, 1986), pp. 33 ff.

2. H. A. Williams, *Some Day I'll Find You* (Fount Paperback, 1984), p. 353.

Chapter 19

1. *The Kabir Book, Forty-four of the Ecstatic Poems of Kabir, Versions by Robert Bly* (Boston: Beacon Press, 1977), p. 1.

2. Kabir, p. 40.

3. Kabir, p. 57.

4. Jacob Needleman, *Lost Christianity* (New York: Doubleday, 1980), pp. 220–222.